T0195929

Ashia's Gift

A Journey Of Smiles And Tears

PLEASANT SMITH

BALBOA.PRESS

A DIVISION OF HAY HOUSE

Balboa Press books may be ordered through booksellers or by contacting:

Balboa Press
A Division of Hay House
1663 Liberty Drive
Bloomington, IN 47403
www.balboapress.com
1 (877) 407-4847

Because of the dynamic nature of the Internet, any web addresses or links contained in this book may have changed since publication and may no longer be valid. The views expressed in this work are solely those of the author and do not necessarily reflect the views of the publisher, and the publisher hereby disclaims any responsibility for them.

The author of this book does not dispense medical advice or prescribe the use of any technique as a form of treatment for physical, emotional, or medical problems without the advice of a physician, either directly or indirectly. The intent of the author is only to offer information of a general nature to help you in your quest for emotional and spiritual well-being. In the event you use any of the information in this book for yourself, which is your constitutional right, the author and the publisher assume no responsibility for your actions.

Any people depicted in stock imagery provided by Getty Images are models, and such images are being used for illustrative purposes only. Certain stock imagery © Getty Images.

Print information available on the last page.

ISBN: 978-1-9822-4119-3 (sc)
ISBN: 978-1-9822-4121-6 (hc)
ISBN: 978-1-9822-4120-9 (e)

Library of Congress Control Number: 2020900330

Balboa Press rev. date: 01/10/2020

Contents

Acknowledgements

To my father Duberick (Luther) Smith as early as I can remember you were battling schizophrenia, but you have never lack being my dad. Your dedication and your love for all your kids were extraordinary. To my kids Worrell, Floyd, Keyshawn and Georgia-nae, you are my source of energy, everything that I had overcome, and everything that I am, happen because God has uses you to bless my life. To all my family members and friends, thank you for your encouragement and support.

My dear Ashia, if you're reading this letter, it could only mean that you're twenty-one years old, so first let me wish you a happy wonderful birthday.

You have been a source of blessing to our lives from the time of your birth and you in turn have been surrounded by love. Because of you Ashia, your mother had a reason to fight in order to hold on to life as long as she did simply so that she can be with you, and so you could also remember her.

You left us when you were only seven, and I haven't seen or heard from you since the day your father said it was best for everyone not to stay in touch. Your father had said that this remaining half of your life would be better lived nonexistent since your mother isn't going to be a part of it in any way. He had said this because the experience or memory you have will slowly fade and he was adamant that you forget your first home clearly stating that the environment wasn't good enough for you anymore.

Now, that you have grown up, I can only imagine the beautiful woman that you've become because after all, you've been blessed with your mothers' warmth and lovely smile, her hazel brown eyes, and your father's straight nose and dark brown hair. It also seems that you were going to have his height, notwithstanding the fact that your mommy wasn't short either my dear.

I hope that when reading this, you will shed some light on any unanswered questions that you might have and with pictures and special gifts (memoirs from your mother). I hope these will bring some closure and peace to your life.

My grandchild, I wish I could tell you to read and enjoy, but I would be lying because with bittersweet memories I write, and with laughter and tears I want you to experience these feelings because this is your past, your present, your future…Your very existence.

I wished I wasn't the one to have written this, but there was no one else to tell you your mother's story, and most importantly she would have wanted me to tell you everything about her. So, I have to grant her this desire despite all odds because my love for her is immeasurable. Carter and I had agreed that it would be the responsibility of either of us that you received your legacy, so when he passed away five years ago, I completed it and sent it to this law firm since I didn't know how much longer I would be able to follow it up. But I hope and pray that I'm still around to see my Celia's daughter one last time, but for now there is a lot for you to discover and a lot to learn, so please read and understand, love and kisses Grandma Theresa.

Chapter One

Welcoming Celia

After what seemed like hours of waiting, I could clearly remember the very day when Celia entered our lives. This was a moment that both I and my husband were eagerly anticipating. When she entered the waiting area, she looked just like the picture that we had received a few days before. She was about 5'6"tall of dark complexion with Afro braids, medium built, but much prettier in person. I don't know if it was the smile she saw on our faces that made her run over to meet us, but at nineteen years old she radiated excitement like a ten-year-old at the ice cream stand.

We hugged each other for what seems like forever while I asked her all these questions at once how was your flight, how did it feel being on an airplane for the first time, how is your mother.......

I would have continued, but my husband put his hand on my shoulder and whispered "hon, you will get as much time to ask all the questions later, but for now let's go home".

I allowed him pick up her single piece of luggage while he led us out of the terminal to the car. Before we moved off, she had turned and looked at me and said "Auntie I am happy to be here and thank you for taking me to live with you, I will not disappoint you."

I felt so much compassion towards her, and was moved to say "I love you my dear, and I know you will not disappoint us". "I can speak for my husband as well that we are blessed to have you in our lives, our home has become too quiet". We held hands as we exited the airport lobby and headed over to the car in the parking lot.

I told Celia to sit in the front passenger seat beside Carter so she can view as much of the scenery on our way home. We were all enjoying the sights as we started answering her many questions.

It was a lovely sunny day with a cool breeze in New York in mid-July. The sky was clear with temperatures in the 70 degrees Celsius range. Carter my husband was laughing because of something Celia had said when I drifted into thoughts as a result of which I didn't hear, but at that very moment, I knew so well that our life would never again be the same.

After three years of loneliness in our house, Carter and I would actually be sharing our home again and we had thought that it was about time we did. Our only son Craig had died tragically along with his wife and two kids in an airplane crash and it was soon to be fourth anniversary since the occurrence of that tragic experience that we would never forget.

We had expected them to return home after their two week long vacation, but they had decided to leave their car at the airport so that they could drive themselves home. Craig had declined our offer to take them to and from the airport, and they insisted that they didn't want to be a burden to us because of the scheduled time of the flight.

They were to land late that afternoon, so his father Carter and I had prepared dinner while we waited for them to arrive before we ate. Carter had gone into the living room and turned on the television and I had just about finished setting the table when I heard a loud wail from him. Rushing into the living room, I looked at him, and his face was so pale as though all the blood had drained from it. He seemed to be in deep shock as he continued to stare blankly at the TV screen.

I followed his gaze to the TV, then I saw the breaking news scrolling across the screen and seeing what looked like an airplane on fire on the runway with firefighters and ambulances. Then came the moment family members dreaded when the flight number, the airplane wreckage were revealed and everything became a blur. The plate I was holding fell from my hands, hit the floor and clattered in pieces across the room. I also felt dizzy and felt myself collapsing. I felt my husband hands catching me and suddenly everything went blank.

When I woke up, there were other voices but when I heard Theresa, I knew that was your grandpa, but when my eyes fluttered opened I saw two other faces; they were the paramedics. Mrs Daniels "could you please respond, if you're hearing?" I nod, and one answer, "Glad to have you back." Carter was smiling with sadness in his eyes whence he told me I had scared him for a minute, but I knew that wasn't true because the paramedics wouldn't have been there that quickly. I later noticed that I was in our living room on the couch, so I asked Carter what had happened and how long since I had been out, he told me that it was about fifteen to twenty minutes, and then I remembered. Like a jolt of current I sprang out of the couch, but the paramedics and Carter caught me and forced me to lie back down, the television set was off at the time but I was crying and asking for my kids and my grandkids, insisting that I want to go see them and know where they were, but Carter was sitting there on the couch beside me just shaking his head. I really needed to know what was going on, but nobody was saying anything.

The paramedics that were checking my vitals told me that I need to relax because my blood pressure was high and so they had to take care of me first. Monitoring my condition at that moment they wanted to take me to the hospital for observation before they can talk about the accident. But I didn't want to go to the hospital, all I cared to know about at that moment were our children, so I stopped crying and mustered up

3

the strength to give them a few minutes to continue checking on me, then with pleading eyes I turned to my husband and said "Honey where are our kids, I want to know?" He then looked at the paramedics who nodded at him in accordance, and then looked back at me, in reality, I could tell what had happened as I could see it in his eyes, but my mind was in denial and I needed to hear it. There wasn't any survivor based on the impact of the crash more especially from the fire I guess.

The next thing I knew was that I woke up in the hospital, I could clearly see that there were persons in white and smelling different scents. I realized that they were shining a light in my eyes while moving a finger from one side to another, and a doctor was saying "Stay with us Mrs. Daniels, you keep on going into unconsciousness," so I wink my eyes and when they had finally finished, they left the room. Carter and his sister and her husband came into the room, but despite the fact that I was the patient in the hospital bed, my heart sank when I saw my husband and I wished that I could change places with him because everything had totally changed as he looked ten years older. I stretched out one of my hands to him and slowly pulled him towards me on the bed, he lowered his head to my face and we hugged, and I whispered in his ears and told him that I was being selfish and that I will never leave him again. I assured him that we are in this together, as our kids are now gone.

He made me know that he is aware of the whole drama and told me that I gave him a worse scare because he felt like I was leaving him too, which put him in a state of anxiety because he don't think he could survive. He then kissed me and lay next to me on the bed while we talked briefly with his family because we were both exhausted. When they were ready to leave, they offered to drive my husband home but he refuses, saying that he will be staying with me there in the hospital for the night, and as a result of being sedated I was already drifting off.

When I woke up the next morning, Carter was still sleeping while he was lying on the couch next to my bed snoring slightly looking a bit peaceful, but his posture looked restless as if he hadn't slept in weeks, then I rested my head back onto the pillow, closed my eyes and drifted off. I had gotten pregnant two times before Craig and both were girls, but there were complications and I had miscarriage. We tried a few years after but not successful, then five years had passed and we hadn't come close to getting pregnant. I was in my early thirties while he was ten years older than me, but yet no children. We had just thought about giving up, but a miracle happened. It was five years since my last pregnancy and I had gotten pregnant again. I tried to be careful as possible for both of us because we couldn't manage another loss, but we are a people of faith and this time there weren't any complications because this baby boy was as healthy as a horse right up to the nine months. He was definitely a blessing in our lives an added joy to our relationship. Surrounded by our family and the church family, we raised him up in the church and had taken him seriously through school. While pursuing his career in journalism, he met and married someone in our church and although they were in their mid-twenties and they were goal-oriented.

They were living in an apartment when they got married, but after they became pregnant with their first child, they decided to look for something bigger, so I talked him into moving in our house because it was so big with only me and his father living in it. When we bought that house, it was for a family of at least five because Carter and I love kids very much, so we had intended to have a few. We talked him to move back in so that we could get the chance to help in raising our grandchild or children, three years after they give birth to their second son, we were so happy and excited to raise our grandchildren and have a lively house, while watching them grow up. Their last son had just turned four

5

years old when they decided that they needed a family vacation which happened to be their first family vacation, so they decided to go to the Caribbean and we were all excited about this trip because they would definitely make some memories, one that they would all remember.

We kept in touch daily as we sent pictures and did life videos, all though they were very happy enjoying themselves but we missed them so much. We were actually counting down the days of their return and now why, what, how can they not be coming back? We had conditioned our mind and heart for two weeks, but eventually got a lifetime heartbreak, as tears flowed down I started to talk to God for the strength and faith to continue.

We got home and I didn't even realize that we had reached. Honey; I became suddenly aware that he had held the door open,I smile and he help me got out of the car, Celia was already out of the car staring at the house in awe. With a board grin she turned to me and said "Really, auntie is this your house and is this where I'll be living, in such a huge lovely house? I said to her "Yes, this is where we will be living? She had reached the door and was waiting for me and Carter to come open the door, so that she can go inside.

The front door opened up into a large open foyer with half spiral stairs that led upstairs to the five bedrooms and bathrooms, it also has the master suite with two balconies and a study room. Downstairs consists of the living and dining room, a breakfast room and a large kitchen, a half bath and powder room, and the library while the basement consists of the gym, laundry room and a helper's quarters. The back of the house has a gazebo, a patio and the pool, and two large garages at the side of the house. Celia had her mouth wide open in huge surprise throughout the entire tour.

By the time we had finished with the site seeing, the take out that Carter ordered had arrived so there was much so catching up to do around the dining table. Celia was filling us in on what was happening back at home, and being the oldest of five siblings, she had life difficulties especially when her father the only breadwinner of the family died a year ago as a result of which she had wanted to quit high school, but we had gone to the funeral and saw the ugly conditions my sister and her kids were living in and that's when me and your grandpa decided to be fully responsible for Celia and her expenses to grow through high school, and then we would take her to live with us so that she could finish school, get a job and help her mother with her siblings. They didn't have much, but you could see that they were loving and helpful to each other, after dinner, we tidied the place and decided to go to bed early.

It was about half an hour later when I heard the door knock, I was a little bit startled because we haven't heard our door knock for such a long time, so I invited her in but she slightly popped her head in and told Carter and I good night with a shy smile and an 'I love you.' We both chorused our goodnight and an 'I love you' back that night as I drifted off to sleep in my husband arms. I felt both our bodies relax while listening to his breathing rhythm as I snuggled closer. I know we were going be alright I believe the Lord has given us a second chance.

It was busy the rest of the week as we went shopping a few days, purchasing, unpacking and organizing her room so that she could settle in and feel at home before the weekend arrives. We attended church and our church family friend gave her a warm welcome, and that very day in church the young people ministry had put on a play so we had spent the entire day at church. She loves church so much because her parents made it compulsory that they all attended church activities, as a result of which she was active in the youth ministry and was also a part of the choir. This was her kind of environment and in no time, she immediately fit right in and became an added asset to the choir with her melodic voice.

Those early months were active; we put a plan into action first by getting her accustomed to driving on the road, so she got her license on the first road test and then a part-time job while she enrolled to do a certified nursing assistant. It was her choice of career, but since I was a retired registered nurse I would be there to help her as much as she needed. She was focused and determined to accomplish her goal, so for over a year she balanced her job, going to school, activities around the house and church. She looked so exhausted after the whole stress, so I tried talking her out of slowing down and even tried getting her to give up the part-time job because we felt she wasn't in need of the money. So Carter and I decided to cover her expenses, but she kept telling us that she could manage because the money she works for was sent home to her mother in order to help cover her siblings school expenses because two of them were in high school, and she had promised them that she will see to it that they graduated.

When her father had died of lung cancer, money absence became very high which was the deciding factor to quitting school since she was the eldest of her siblings. Carter and I had found this out from my sister when I asked her what she planned to do to support herself and the kids, she told me that there were some savings and life insurance at her husband's job that she will manage with until she got a job. So we made the decision to be fully responsible for Celia.

It was a few months before her final exams, so we begged her again to give that job up and only focus on her studies, but she was determined to continue so we chose to respect her decision and just give her the support when she needed it. That day of her final exam, we prayed together and she became very confident in herself; we believed in her too. So, when she arrived home there was a broad grin on her face; she had passed her finals her which paid off as a result of her determination.

Some of the young people at church with the help of my husband and I planned a surprise celebration party at a bowling alley, we took care of the whole expense so that they could all enjoy themselves perfectly.

That weekend, when she saw the new car we bought her she was lost for words, Carter and I love her as our own because she fills that empty place in our hearts that only a child of our own could fill.

Chapter Two

Her Diagnose

It had been about two years since Celia started working at the hospital and found it to be a second home and family because she loved her job so much and her co-workers. It was less than fifteen minutes driving from the house which caused her to do a lot of extra hours at work because her five years plan is to go back home and buy her mother a bigger house than what they were living in, and she was also helping her out more financially because her mother still wasn't working yet.

It was a week before her twenty sixth birthday that she introduced us to Phillip, but it wasn't a surprise because we knew she was dating. We trusted that she will know if he is actually the one for her and whenever she is ready, we will get to meet him. He was four years older and seems disciplined, definitely an extrovert, and opposite of your mother, but they seem to get on just fine because they were in love with each other.

His first time at the house was for dinner; his features was highly presentable as he was seen pulling out the chair for Celia at the table and he even offered to grace the dinner table. When he was addressing your Grandfather, it was Mr. Daniels or Sir and when it was me, it was

Mrs. Daniels or ma'am. He holds a conversation during dinner by the evening telling each other a lot about themselves and life in general which got Carter and I impressed and intrigued as we had learned a lot about him too.

He was a Canadian by birth but had relocated some years back and attended college here in the USA as an only child. When his father died his mother needed a change so she accepted a position to work and live in the state. They would return home very often because all their family members were there. He is employed at the same hospital where she works and shared an apartment with his best friend.

After meeting him, we approved of their relationship because he and your mother were inseparable as they went everywhere together. He left his church and started attending our church which made her so happy, while Carter and I were grateful to God that we had made the right decision to take her into our lives. She had indeed fulfilled her promise, and she was doing her best every day moving forward, it was quite amazing.

They were going steady for about one year when Philip proposed to her. That day when they came over by the house, Carter was in the family room watching sports and I was in the study taking care of some bills, she came and knocked on the door, so when I looked up from the decks she asked if I was busy, then I told her that I was almost finished and I'll be with her in five minutes.

Philip was in the family room with Carter, so she will just wait out there until I am through. After a few minutes, I went into the family room whence I met Carter and Philip talking about sports, but Celia was sitting with her eyes closed with her back head resting against the sofa. I instantly felt something was off, still having my eyes on her I saw the ring on her finger, she was engaged and it was obvious. I took a seat beside Carter and said; you kids now have our full attention. So she sat up on the sofa and Phillip put his hand on her lap as they looked at us from across the room. Celia lifted up her left hand to show us the ring but Philip was the one to speak. Excitedly but nervous they announced their engagement as they both walked across to us. Carter and I stood and hugged, and congratulated them both while expressing how happy we are and we hope for the best and they will always be in our prayers.

We saw that they are in love and also a perfect fit, after a few more hugs we are all sat down.

Celia was still silent, so I asked if there was something else she needed to tell us, she replied 'yes auntie' here is some more news it was right then that I knew what was going on, and so I had to ask her how far was her pregnancy and she told us that she was three weeks late and that they had already done the test, which confirmed that she was indeed pregnant.

She wasn't that excited because she hadn't told Phillip that she had a health problem as we had instructed her to do months before. She promised us that she would tell him of her condition when was sure they have a future together. But she became pregnant and he had proposed, and she still holds the secret away from him. Philip was pretty excited telling us that they want to get the marriage plans done in a month from that very day because he didn't want the preparation of the baby birth to take up their time and energy plus they will need to search for an apartment of their own.

When he realizes that Celia wasn't talking, he started making excuse for her by telling us that she was just as happy, but she hadn't planned and getting pregnant right, but stating clearly that it wasn't because of the baby that he has proposed to her that he knew from the first time he met her that she was his wife. He just kept talking and my husband and I just sat there listening because we know exactly what was going on with Celia, we helped to grow her so we could her. It was so obvious that he was left in the dark after he had finally finished talking about his plan. We reassure him that the house will basically be Celia's one day, so they can start making arrangements to occupy a section of the house, and as for the wedding we are fully on board because we want our daughter to get the wedding she dreamt of while her expense is totally on us and a month planning sounds very fine.

Less than a week after their announcement my phone rang, it was Phillip calling while inquiring to know if we were at home. Celia has just given him the news of her illness, and he wants us to explain more to him so that he can fully understand. There wasn't much more to tell, but we told him they should come over to the house that we will be waiting.

Celia had basically educated him about her diagnosis and we told him that it was in her final year of study that we noticed how most times she looked drain and we would try hard to get her to take care of herself, but she was always pushing, we were just praying for the time to come quickly so that she could be done with school and get a job in her field of study, and thereby create some time to take better care of herself.

One night when we were in bed, Carter had asked me if I had noticed anything different with her, I said I have but I am hoping that all the stress would be over so that she could come back to her normal self, he said it seems physically she is present but her mind always seems to be wondering.

Sometimes you would be talking to her but she won't respond, and it's after you call her name most times that she would jump on her feet and apologize. I told him about a particular day in which she couldn't find her car keys and how she got very agitated when it seemed that she couldn't remember where she had put them which was unlike her.

We talked about other minor things because we believed that something was definitely wrong somewhere and so we decided to watch her keenly for a few more days now that she had our attention, but after the following day we decided to carry her to the doctor. She had to take up a book to study, but wasn't really looking into it rather she was talking softly to herself despite having the book in front of her.

The doctor got us fixed for an afternoon visit, but as the time past I was talking to God and I kept telling myself that there is nothing to worry about. She is just fine, it was only overwork, stress, and lack of sleep, the study of her job and the missing of her family. She was dwelling in a new environment and so she needed time adjust to the changes, but most importantly she was pretty young.

She used to work-out on a regular no wonder her body and the mind had been in serious overdrive. I continue to talk to God while on our way to see the doctor, I asked God to heal, bless and strengthen her. The doctor has partly agreed with us that the amount of stress she has undergone can be drastic to her health and her well-being, so he ran a number of tests on her but he didn't rule out anything that very day because he suggested to have her on evaluation along with the findings on those tests.

She had her upcoming exams, so he prescribed mild medication and suggested that she get the well-deserved rest for him to have the right diagnosis at her next visit with a warning that she needs to take herself out of whatever causes the stress. She was on medication and also on sick leave before her exams, after which everything seemed to be alright and after a few days, she was back to her normal self again. She had mastered her exams and officially became a certified nurse.

When we revisited the doctor, he was so impressed with the result but decided to keep her on mild medication, and continued to monitor her progress. He also informed us that she even might one day stop using medication, but she has to play her part by taking good care of herself, avoid stress, get proper rest to eat well and exercise and she will most likely heal.

After about six months, the doctor took her off prescription meds and she was able to purchase over the counter drugs if she feels she needed to relax, but stated that he must have her in every three months for a consultation visit, he even suggested that she should avoid anything that might tip her health because of the delicate situation.

Getting pregnant was one of those tips, she should have had a medical done before planning to get pregnant. So, we made Phillip to clearly understand that that was the reason why she didn't seem happy about the baby because she is afraid of what might go wrong with her or the baby. We made him know how much she loves kids because she practically helped in raising all her siblings but as of that moment, she will be needing all the support and rest she can get. This was a guarantee, and because they will be living with us it will make things much easier on her, as we will be there for her 100%. We are going to see that she takes good care of herself and the baby.

Her wedding was on a Tuesday afternoon in the church and the young adult volunteered to do decorations, so we had to pay for a private catering service and location. It had a little over a hundred people attend the wedding, some of his close relatives had arrived from Canada, our relatives and some of the church family and Celia's mom also had come for the wedding too. It was a very beautiful wedding with her in that lovely princess dress with crystal bodice and crown vail, two bridesmaids and her best friend from church, Jean, was her maid of honor. Phillip's best friend Patrick was his best man, and also participating were two of his cousins from Canada.

They left the day after the wedding for their honeymoon in Ontario, Canada, for a four-day stay at a wonderful hotel that his mother had booked for them, and she was very excited it had been her first trip since coming to live in the states. She had never gone to Canada before, so she would enjoy the trip while getting the chance to meet more of Phillip's relatives and to make some lovely memories. She took numerous pictures and short videos for you and that's when the memoirs started. She returned home happy and content to be a wife and a mother.

They had comfortably moved in as husband and wife, so we had helped them get settled in with Phillip's mother help too. Carter was especially glad now that he had a sports buddy to relax with it, and he was friendly and easy-going, but I would always excuse them and get busy or rather go for shopping whenever they were watching a game and vouching for opposing team.

The months following up to the delivery date went smoothly as she followed up on all her doctor's appointments with either your dad or me accompanying her. It was really exciting going on shopping for baby stuffs and even more excited when decorating the nursery in pink white and lavender, and also arranging so much pretty girly stuffs as we already knew it was a girl. Those were the loveliest moments for her with the exception of morning sickness, a huge belly and a bloated body, she was doing pretty fine.

She continued to take pictures and do small videos, then I could sense that it was more for what might have happened rather than for memories sake. We were just about finishing up a few adjustments because she has less than two weeks to her due date, she sighs while we were talking as she sat in the armchair rocking slowly. Then I asked her if she was tired because she had only been a week since she had stopped working, she answered no but there was something else she wants to say to me which was very important to her.

I stopped what I was doing, looked at her and noticed fear moving in her eyes, then she asked that I made her a promise that if anything happens to her before or after the baby was born, I should help Phillip raise her, she explained that the last thing she would want is to put her daughter in danger of any sort because of the possibility of what might happen according to the doctor.

I told her that she's going to be fine and that we'll continue to pray and trust God for his blessings. I went over and hugged her, but I knew she was still worrying so I told her to take good care of herself and focus on getting that lovely baby into the world and anything after that we will deal with it accordingly, and with a little relief she smiled and agreed.

That Sunday morning it was business as usual but it was her due day, so we stayed at home and didn't bother to go to church so as to give her support and help her to relax until she feels she needs to go into the hospital. During her pregnancy, she had a craving for salty food and so that morning after eating one of her favorite breakfasts that consists of fritters with codfish beacon and orange juice, she vomited everything which happened to be the first time she did that ever since she got pregnant. We did make fun of it that she was finally counting downtime, but she wasn't actually feeling any pain.

On that particular day, Carter and I had prepared dinner so she could eat, and it got to about five in the afternoon when she started feeling the cramp, so we brought her to the hospital in less than twenty minutes away.

It was where both of them worked, so we knew for sure that she would be well taken care of as they had been expecting her. So everything went smoothly in a few minutes, and after arriving she was settled in the room while your father stayed with her and Carter and I stayed in the waiting area, while we were there Claudette arrived and by seven o'clock that evening you were born; a healthy baby girl who weighed eight and three-quarter pound.

We stayed a while with our reverend along with his wife, and two of your mother's close friends also visited while we were there. When we finally left for home your father stayed behind to bring her and the baby home the following day.

He had taken leave from work to stay home with Celia and you for two weeks, although he had no siblings and did not know anything about newborn but yet, he was very attentive and caring. In a very short time, he was changing diapers and clothes, feeding and burping, and a bit more relax when holding you. Your mommy did take some amusing pictures of him having these lovely moments.

In just a month she had everything under control with the experience she had while helping to raise her siblings. However, Carter and I were happy to babysit while she was doing small chores such as doing the laundry, preparing the baby stuff and minor errands.

They had also made plans with Reverend to have you christened when you were three months old, they had Carter and I appointed guardian and Godparents for you, and Phillip's best friend, Patrick, was one of the Godfathers and Celia best friends, Jean was one of the GodmothersCelia and you were both wearing white that day, she had hired a professional photographer for the service, and afterwards we went home with the few family members and close friends. The buffet was catered on the patio near the pool area; it was such a wonderful day. Celia was so happy with her adorable daughter, so she finally returned to work the next day and Carter and I was left to take care of you, we were excited to help raise our granddaughter.

On your first birthday, Celia had gone all out. It was Doc Miss McStuffins team that she invited with about thirty other people, kids, and adults also included was another outdoor event at the house in which she had ordered two cakes a very small one with a single candle, and after you blew it out you made a mess with your hands on it.

Celia's mother had come from Jamaica for the first time to be with her grandchild, so she plans on spending four months with us and was to stay for Christmas.

One day while we were decorating the house, Phillip was at work, you were with Celia's mother, Mavis, in the nursery. Carter was outside with the Landscaper more likely keeping up his time in conversation which we could never tell him because he always thinks that doing a little bit of raking was working so however, it does keep him occupied. Looking through the window at him giving a belly out laugh, I smile and wondered what had got him as he now talks basically anything with the landscaper from politics, religion, current affairs but especially sport.

He was about twenty years older than Carter, but as long as somebody is available to talk about the game they were Carter's friend even if they were on the opposite side. It wouldn't matter to him having a conversation with Horace because it was always fun and interesting, and at his age and experience he basically doesn't take much seriously. He had to find humor in everything and gratitude in his blessings although we lost our family tragically, but his support still teaches me to accept what we have, the opportunities to share, and the lives we were able to touch. The landscaper had being doing our lawns for years, we know about his family and he knows about ours so well.

After the passing of Craig, he was with Carter for hours after he had finished working. Caught up in thoughts I heard when Celia call me, so I turned to her and that's when she told me that Phillip will be leaving for Canada the day after Christmas for a few days and he will be back on New Year's Eve. Surprisingly, I asked her if she didn't feel happy about going with the baby, but her answer was no because your father told her that since he had been married he hadn't enough time with her, and he usually visits home often so he feels he deserves the break.

So her concern was; does having a family not eliminate certain kind of lifestyle from a single one? I told her it does, but how they go about it matters to only the person that is involved which is both of them, and the only way to achieve this is through honesty, effective communication and understanding. I also made her to know that sometimes they will have to agree to disagree, so my advice to her is to speak her true feelings about it to him and see how it goes. Because Mavis was there and she would be going back to Jamaica on New Year's Eve, Celia got busy between working and shopping with her, and also for Christmas. She hadn't talked about the outcome of speaking with her husband, but we know for certain that he was still going to Canada on his trip.

We all go to church together for the early morning service, Carter's sister and her family was also visiting along with two of his brothers which made the house full and festive; the excitement of conversation, foods, and drinks a lovely day.

However, the brother's trip was very short as they went back to Florida the next day, they didn't like the weather but the following year would be our turn to visit them for Christmas and of course, our visit usually lasts for at least a week because we love the weather there.

That morning when Phillip was leaving for Canada, Carter took him to the airport then you and I were to go with your mother and grandmother that afternoon. They had a couple of hours before we would be leaving and Carter returned as he was very concerned if everything was okay with Phillip and Celia because to him Phillip seems as though he was under some sort of pressure, which could cause him to easily get distracted. I didn't fully understand what was going on, but I told him the little that I had heard from Celia.

Shortly after we took Mavis to the airport it was very emotional for Celia to see her go, your mommy cried because she was dealing with more than the fact that her mother was leaving, but her husband had already left and I know for certain that she wished he hadn't. She promised her mom to visit the new year because she misses her home and it would be the first time going back since she had left five years ago.

On our way back home, she told me of the conversation with her husband stating that she didn't see it as an issue leaving because it's only a few days and it is usually something that he got accustomed to, and whenever Celia wants to visit home with or without him he would be fully supportive of her decision, so she agreed to disagree but she would leave it at that because the only other way is to try to stop him because she couldn't go either, and that would cause tension with them because they both decided to focus on her love for the family and move on, and things will be good when he returns.

But sadly that didn't happen as a matter of fact because Phillip seemed tensed and impatient as if he was under some kind of pressure; he speaks less, they snap at each other more often when you weren't even aware.

The day he returned, his friend Patrick had picked him up from the airport while they were going to the New Year countdown celebration in Manhattan making excuses for her to not wanting to go with him reminding her. She had to work early that morning, but he wasn't due to go back to work for two more days and he will be with some alumni from college. It seems to her that he was deliberately trying to avoid her and his daughter; it was obvious that he spent all his time off away from them. She was becoming frustrated with his behaviors.

New Year's morning, some driver had dropped him off at an unknown house and your mother woke us up startled. We rushed with her to find out that your father had puked and passed out on the bathroom floor in most of the liquor. We tried to get him to respond but he was too drunk, so the three of us has to get him cleaned up, clothed him and laid him in bed. Celia had work to do in a few hours while stating that she was going to call in her absence, but we urged her to go and assured her that your grandfather would keep an eye on her husband and if anything comes up, we will rightfully inform her. She still looked worried while she was leaving. He was still sleeping when she called four hours later, but it was late in the afternoon that he finally woke up. We were in the kitchen fixing dinner when he walked in while rubbing his ear temple. I fixed him a cup of tea to drink, so when I suggested something to eat he declined stating that his stomach was too sore to eat anything. I asked him about the previous night, but he couldn't recall anything, not even about the taxi, nor the mess, and surely not the part that Carter and I undressed him, cleaned him up and struggled to put him in bed. Having heard the details from me got him so embarrassed, but I had to let him know how I felt about his actions.

He was very apologetic, stating that it's unlike him and he can actually count on one hand the number of times he had ever gotten drunk and that was in college. It didn't go well with me, so I made him understand that abusing liquor in order to get over whatever is bothering him isn't going to solve it. I thought that he needed to talk to his wife because we all knew there was more going on with him before he damages his relationship and hurt his family. Certain changes occurred and it was very evident that it was taking a toll on Celia. He was told to always remember her condition and know that whatever happens will affect his daughter, so he finally left saying that he was going to call and apologize to her and afterwards to check on you in the nursery. That evening when she reached home from work, she looked so drained that I asked her if she might need to see her doctor, but she told me that she had some meds which she has been taking for about two weeks on. She also said that she had told her doctor about her current condition and got a prescription from him afterwards.

I wasn't aware that few months earlier the doctor had told her that if she felt the same after her meds had finished she should call and set an appointment to see him or she could wait on her upcoming appointment. She explained to me that she only needs to take a shower, eat and get some rest, so we hugged and said goodnight after she had finished eating.

I didn't see her again until the following morning as they were both on their day off. They took you along with them to a birthday party that one of Celia co-worker was having for her daughter. They were both in a better spirit and looked much better than the previous day as they left the house early in order to have lunch before going for the party.

Chapter Three

Returning Home

T he next couple of weeks went smoothly as they were doing certain things together as a family and as a couple, and they equally took you to the park, the mall, the aquarium and practically any fun places for kids.

They went for dinner, to the movies, they went bowling. Ever since you were born, Celia stopped going to the gym, so she re-activated her membership at the gym and the both of them started going together and visiting church, as usual, it was lovely to see that they found pleasure in themselves once again. It was Valentine's Day and she was happy, so she came home that evening with flowers, a gift and an invitation to a romantic evening at a five star hotel. That was the first time Celia left you overnight, and on the fifth of the week before was the day that they would have celebrated their first wedding anniversary, but they decided on doing it on valentine's days which your mother was extremely excited about and confessed that it was a perfect idea. Both Carter and I was happy to care for you till they returned home the following afternoon.

In a couple of months around the end of spring, Carter and I had booked a two week vacation, this was a senior retreat that his brother had gone to a few times before and urged us to give it a try, and after we would spend another two weeks at his house in Florida.

A vacation for us was well overdue, so we decided to go and we would return in time to help in making arrangements and to celebrate your two years old birthday party.

It had been a lovely two week vacation, we enjoyed every minute of it having Carter's brother and wife there, and they even got us to reach an agreement on doing it again the following year.

Two days before we were due to return home, my phone rung while we were sleeping though it wasn't that late, but it was frightening when I saw that it was Phillip and not Celia calling. I became anxious so I asked him about your mommy and if you were okay, he told me that you were sleeping but he was stumbling on his words trying to explain about Celia. When I asked again he noticed that I was getting impatient so he hesitated a few seconds and then slowly answered that she was not fine. He told me that lately she had been less expressive and aloft, and sometimes even unaware of what she is doing but it didn't last for long, and when he talked her into telling me about it she would say she was okay simply because she didn't want to have us worrying unnecessarily. She had already told me that she was on the mild doze and so he offered to bring her to the doctor, but she told him it's best to wait because the appointment date was coming up soon that she only needs to get more rest, I was shocked to be hearing this.

At this time Carter had woken up and was listening, so he offered to see if we could get an early flight out but your father begged us not to, stating that Claudette was helping out with you while we were away. He said that he had called her and she promised to go by and spend the two days at the house until we returned, he wasn't planning on ruining our trip. He assured us that he will be able to do his best until we returned, but what prompted him to call us, was that earlier that evening when he arrived home the place was in total darkness and what frightened him most was that Celia was there sitting in the dark in the living area and no sign of the baby. He called her but she didn't answer, so he went into the nursery to find you sleeping in the crib. Luckily, the night light was always on, so when he saw the condition that you were in, he knew that something was really wrong because you had the same clothes on when he was leaving for work which was already messy with baby food, and your diaper was soaking wet; that was unlike your mother.

He had to take you out, changed everything and put you back to bed. During this time Celia hadn't come into the nursery, to his surprise when he returned to the living area she was still crunched up in the sofa, but now she was talking to herself. At first, he had thought that she was on the cell phone, but when he turned the lights on there wasn't a phone nearby and she was looking at him as if she was seeing him for the first time. She obviously didn't even realize that he was home, so he took her to their bedroom to give her medication and asked if she was hungry, but she had told him no and so he waited until she was asleep and that's when he called us.

He told us that he would set an appointment for the afternoon on the day we will reach, and our flight would be slated to come early so we would be there to take her to the doctor, we agreed and said our good nights and also promised to talk again in the morning.

The day we arrived, Phillip picked us up at the airport with Celia, and the four of us went to the doctor. Claudette was taking care of you and you were staying at her house. Phillip explained Celia's behavior to the doctor, stating that she seems loss of what she was doing and also where she was, but it doesn't last long as it goes quickly like synapses. She was also less energetic, no emotions or feelings, but he kept quiet because your mother didn't want him to say anything.

The first time it happened, he didn't realize that it could get worse and he doesn't understand much about people with schizophrenia. Her doctor ran some tests and prescribed medication and told us that she will be fine, just let her stay away from stressful situations, so he set an appointment to have an earlier visit than usual and gave us a list of therapists we should make an appointment with so as to have her speak with someone.

She didn't go to work for a few days as she had taken sick leave, so we monitored her progress with the medication. What she does mostly was isolate herself, but I told myself that she was just trying to get herself custom of having a family and fitting it into her space. I had also convinced myself that she was adapting to this new life being very young with a family of her own.

Your mom and dad had decided to go to Jamaica to spend a week with you so that Celia's family could know their niece or cousin. They planned to keep your birthday there with reasons that a change of scenery would uplift her spirit and visiting home might be the recipe for her to relax and up her energy level once more.

Celia and I went shopping and planning for the trip. We wanted to keep her busy, but not to the point of allowing her to become exhausted. So over the weeks leading up to the vacations, she continued with her regular routine work, church activities and taking care of her family. Sticking to her medication brought down her behavior to normal as ever.

We were all emotional when she was leaving that day for their vacation because it had been years since she had left, and a lot has changed ever since she got married. Despite being a mother and a career woman, she still attended church activities and doing wonders on the choir. She even planned on expanding in that area, but she was waiting for you to grow a few more years so as to take up singing as an added profession.

She had both accomplished a lot and overcame a lot too, more so yet that she has a lot to give God thanks for.

We hugged again before they left then I wished them a safe journey, she smiled and told me that I need not to worry that she will definitely be coming back home. I replied telling her that their main purpose is to go and enjoy them self, but whatever time she needs to relax she should do so and make memories for herself, her husband, visit exciting places and you; that's all that matters as I'll be waiting for my pictures and video chat.

The time they spent on their vacation were certainly about enjoyment, we received pictures of Dunn's River Falls, Bob Marley Museum, Rose Hall Great House, Green Grotto Cave, but my favorites were the pictures taken at the birthday party. They took the shots at Hamilton Plantation with all the decorations and kiddy's activities, it was an outdoor event all fun and filled with so much excitement. Her eldest brother Paul was the DJ of the day playing all the great music, there was much drinks as there was food and of course one of the biggest loveliest birthday cake. I can honestly say that the trip was well worth it.

When they returned from their trip, it was a joyful moment, as they were happy and relaxed. Celia jokingly asked if I had remembered when she had arrived so scared and nervous, I told her that is was not worth remembering. I could feel that she was excited and was in awe, but she laughed and said that it was the outside appearance, stating that inside of her was nervous and frightened.

Then she began to tell us the story of her visit and laughing so much that caused Carter to look at me, we had to take notice of the fact that she was happy and alive. It was Phillip's first time of visiting the Caribbean but he really loved the experience, and was also planning on going there again because there were a lot of places he didn't get the chance to visit, and a whole lot more activities he didn't get to do before their trip ended.

From the time we left the airport until everyone retired for bed, it was mostly your dad who was occasionally asking for help from Celia and it was mostly when he can't remember a specific name of a person, food, or places even some activities.

Celia and Mavis had planned a family reunion which gave your dad the opportunity to try some traditional food. He was amazed when he got to prove for himself that the country was really about music and food. He was definitely into jerk dishes, Mannish Water that was made with goat meat, and our national dish Ackee and Codfish which was a delicacy that was served with roast breadfruit, but his favorite was the steam fish with okras and crackers wrapped in aluminum foil, Potato Pudding and even some homemade favorites drink. He brought back some souvenirs from Bob Marley Museum, climbed the world famous Dunns River Falls and his first time being in a cave at the Green Grotto caves and also learnt some of the country's history at the Giddy House in Port Royal and the enchanting Rose Hall Great House. His visit was so memorable that he was ready to book his next trip. Celia was so happy to relive some memories even better yet while enjoying everything with you and your father, and they were both relaxed and rested by the time they were back at work a few days later, after which Carter and I resumed our daily chores of taking care of you. Months passed, everything was back to normal or so it seems, until that morning, she brought you over to the house while your grandfather and I were in the kitchen preparing breakfast as it was a Sunday morning routine for both families to sit and eat before leaving for church.

She wasn't dressed but it was still early, so she asked me to let you have breakfast and me to take you to church with me because she wasn't planning on going that day. When I asked her if your dad will be joining us for breakfast or going to Church., she told us no he won't but saying nothing more she excused herself and went to her apartment.

That Sunday morning all three of us ate and then left for church, when we were leaving we noticed that Phillip's car wasn't there as the house has two singles garage, and hers usually parked inside while his parked on the driveway. I was curious but I didn't say anything to Carter although I am sure that he must have noticed it too.

Church was a blessing as usual, the service was powerful coupled with the fact that it was deliverance Sunday, I hoped that your parents had come but I had the Reverend pray a special prayer for them and their relationship. However, when we reached the house that evening to prepare dinner, Celia was in the kitchen and what we normally do is to get some of the preparation out of the way in the morning and finish it after church, so we changed and all had dinner except for Phillip.

She was in a natural mood so we talked about the church service and enjoyed the dinner. Carter and I usually don't interfere when she choose to sort it out personally and whenever she decides to tell us we were always available. When dinner was over, she went to her apartment to have you cleaned up and put you in your pajamas and your grandfather and I would clean up the kitchen pack away leftovers and stock the dishwasher.

It's normal routine for us to meet in the living area, watch the news, and talk about the week events and church, while Phillip and Carter would talk some sports. That evening your dad hasn't showed up, so after about three hours with us your mother took you to bed though it was pretty early for her but she told us good night. When she had left the room, I turned and looked at your grandfather as he put his arm around me and said keep praying it works every time. I snuggled up closer to him and we continued watching the news. Celia was off the following day, so we went to the store to shop for school supplies because you would be starting kindergarten that semester and after spending over three hours in the mall, we picked up lunch and went to the park to eat.

The day was lovely, warm sunshine, birds chirping and flying about picking up whatever crumbs they could get hold of, cool breeze lightly blowing. We sat on the bench, but you hardly ate as you were too excited to play, so we allowed you to enjoy as much of the stuff that you wanted to explore with your favorites being the swing and the slides. We sat there in silence while we ate, but I could sense that her mind was wondering. A few times a parent or guardian she met acquaintance with at the park would wave at her she wave back and smile but she didn't leave the bench.

After what seems like forever, she finally spoke saying "Phillip might not want to come back home to us and I don't feel I will blame him because we hardly speak to each other, and whenever we communicate it's like a routine instead, so it's awfully quiet and lately it seems as if Ashia is the only human being in the house," your mother was talking so low and even though I was hearing what she was saying she wasn't looking at me while she spoke. . I sat in silence and she continued, "I don't want to fight for it." With tears in her eyes she lifted her head looked at me and said "Our marriage?" I reached out and put my hand on her shoulder, "It seems he is unhappy and it has been like this for several months, I am trying to be patient but whenever I reach out to him it feels as if I'm invading his privacy."

She explained that she thought to give him space, but at the moment she doesn't think it's working either because they're only pushing each other apart to the point where the physical separation is presently in play. He had moved out saying it was only for a few days and he is staying by his friend's place Patrick, but she was more worried that suppose after a few days he is still undecided about coming home and instead come for more clothes, days become weeks and he realizes that he truly wants out, then what?

I know she didn't need an answer to that, so I didn't interrupt and she continued to talk stating that she wasn't looking for a perfect relationship because she understands clearly that such doesn't exists. She knew there are days when it feels like all odds is against them as a couple and as an individual, and it takes every ounce of energy to channel the positive into their relationship, but she feels that if the sad times outweighs the happy times and the connection breakdown so bad that one person always have one foot out the door rather than face up to situations when they arrive, then what's the sense? It involves all three for it to work perfectly; the male, the female and relationship. There will be a pull push or imbalance and things will not work out properly if these aren't in alignment. I sat there still in silence understanding that what she needed was my presence and listening ear, she said "Auntie, I have done my research, a lot of reading on relationship and my intention is to be married once, but in reality it takes two."

I know she wasn't finished when she stopped, but she got up and went over to the slide, stretched out her hand to you and caught you and when you slid down to her you were giggling so much. On that day, she took pictures of you wearing the Mickey Mouse pink shorts outfit, she then brought you over to the bobble horse, made you sit on it and tilted it back and forth as if you were riding, and she took more pictures while you giggled with excitement. As I sat there watching her taking you from one area to another making it fun for you, inside her was in turmoil unknown of what the future holds for her family, but at the same time still trying to hold it together which got me heartbroken. She then brought you by the swing to stay there for a while and chit chat with some of the other ladies, so when she returned to where I was on the bench, she put you down but you ran back over to the slide as fast as your tiny feet could carry you. We took a couple more pictures, and for a while both of us were laughing because our minds and focus was all on you. When she sat down she took a deep breath, not from being tired, but a sigh of relief. We looked at each other and then she turned her focus back on you, I could see the fear in her eyes from the way she was fondling her hands in her lap. I put one hand on hers again so she could know that I'm still there with her assuring her of my support always. I was encouraging her that she should not give up, she must continue to pray and have hope because God is still able. She told me that not once had she stopped praying nor lost hope, and she also believed in miracles because that's exactly what she needs to save her family, when she said this I knew there was more to come. She began to tell me that it's not only difference in agreement that is causing problems in their relationship, but her husband seems to be distracted as there are other priorities than his family and she was guessing that it's an affair he was involved in and it could even be before they were married. His mood swing is becoming more obvious and his mind is so preoccupied that only his physical presence seems to be there at home. Lately, they got into a fight the other day before he moved out while he kept threatening her that she better not think that he will leave his daughter with her, and she should not even think about carrying him to court because there is no way that a judge will grant her a schizophrenic custody of you.

When we returned home that evening, his SUV was in the driveway and when we went inside he was there with Carter talking and watching sport. He got up as we were entering the living room, came over and picked you up and put his arm around your mommy and kissed her and told her he misses her and his daughter. She just stood there looking at him in so much confusion, he asked how was I doing and I told him that I was good. The moment was getting awkward then he started to charm himself out by telling us that he had help Carter prepared dinner and they were about to eat because they were starting to think if we are going to return home, ironically that's your style Celia said sarcastically with disgust telling him that no one was expecting him anyhow, she then took you out of his hands and excused herself to have you cleaned up for dinner, he then followed her excusing himself too insisting that he will bath you.

There wasn't much talking at the dinner table that evening as Carter was the only neutral energy because he was the only one who doesn't know most of what was going on. Phillip was trying to act and look sincere, but no one was buying it. Your mother was still upset and it seemed that she started to resent him for his erotic behavior, and one could easily see that she was hurting even more because she can't make sense of what was happening, but I think at that moment he knew that this was the last time he will be able to return if he should pull a stunt like that again. My husband and I would not tolerate that kind of disrespect in our home to our daughter and his immature attitude of leaving his family when he seems fit and returns when he likes was going to end immediately. I was going to wait and see how Celia was going to deal with the situation, and soon after dinner they left for their apartment instead of hanging around to chat which was okay for me because I didn't feel like exchanging polite conversation with Phillip at that moment anyhow.

Chapter Four

Couples coaching

Later that day, I told your granddad what I had learned from Celia at the park but it was upsetting for him and he also told me that he had a talk with Phillip from a man, a father and a husband point of few. He did also ask him what he would do to fix their relationship and save their marriage, and Phillip told him that he had already made recommendations and that the first thing he will be doing is to set an appointment to get professional help, but he will first discuss with Celia to see where they stand because he didn't know if she would even want to stay married to him again. He also said that he was going to apologize and ask for her forgiveness with hopes that she does forgive him, he claimed that he still loves and cares for her and that he wants their marriage to work while stating that he has no intentions of breaking up their family.

I clearly told your grandpa that I didn't believe a word that Phillip said because his actions said a lot about him which is gradually becoming a pattern and I think that there is more going on. Phillip loves the idea of a family life, but he acts as though he is single. They have been married for three years and he had already moved out two times, but for you and your mother sake I was hoping that he would come back to his senses and find a way to fix the damage he caused, and stop putting his family's well being and security on the line. How much can a person take since he already knows and understands the sensitivity of Celia's mental health?

I would prefer he makes a clean break rather than playing with her emotions. It was disgusting to know that he picked up a fight through the door with his 'I'm out of here' attitude and thinks that he could just pick up the charming attitude on his way back in like I got my groove back, so he got me thinking what healthy relationship works that way with one party jumping ship to refuel with no consideration of the next person. I was starting to get upset and your grandfather was beside me trying to get me to calm, but I could only imagine how your mom was feeling.

I was wondering how he does view love. The day after Celia told me that he had set an appointment with a relationship couples coach to start getting the help they needed in order to save their relationship, nothing else mattered to me than to see her happy again but she also told me that she had made it clear to him that if he should ever walk out on his family again, he must leave the divorce papers and sign it because there is no way he could return because the first appointment was in two days. That was a good start because Celia was hardly talking to him; she needed his support, she has been having flare up on and off with her condition even though she was on medication, she tries to hide it by putting the best attitude outside but I knew that she was worrying a lot. The doctor assured us that she wasn't in any situation for stronger meds.

But fully aware of the fragile state that she was in was one of the main reasons why Carter and I wasn't happy with the way your father was behaving knowing fully well that the last thing Celia should be dealing with is stress because this could tip her over the edge and compromise whatever progress she was making although she didn't have much of anything out of her family life and she was active in most parts of the church activities. She had two close friends; one at church who was her maid of honor and the other from her workplace. She and Celia would spend more time with her because she too had two kids; a boy and a girl, her husband was in the navy so she had some amount of free time. Celia and Kerry would make arrangements for play dates for the children and going to the movies, museum or whatever places for kids, so she was her closest friend.

The weekend following the first coaching session, your dad decided to do some barbecue because he was having two of his cousins from Canada visiting. We were also joined by his best friend, his mother and her husband, Celia two friends, their husbands and their children. It was a wonderful day and the sun was hot in the seventies, but the temperature was lovely because it was so windy and there were lots of trees in our area. The men basically were by the grill, but everyone was enjoying the food, the drinks, the pool, and most of all the friendly conversation as everyone had made acquaintance before, so for each other it was a family settings.

Celia took the time to make a short video and I helped her to take pictures of you splashing in the pool with the other kids, when you had ketchup from your hotdog, and barbecue chicken sauce all over your face and hands, when Phillip was blowing bubbles in your face and you were trying to burst as much as possible, and when he was with you in the pool teaching you how to swim; you loved the water so you were giggling so hard and bouncing around because of the floats you had on you and a lot more fun pictures. Everybody had a blast and later offered to help do the cleaning up, and when it was done a few stayed back just relaxing on the patio.

I had noticed that Celia left and didn't return for about ten minutes. She hadn't taken you inside along with her and one of her best friends was still there. So I went about looking for her until I saw her outside by her bedroom porch sitting in a very confused and worrying manner, standing at the door I called her but she didn't open her eyes and didn't even move., I repeat her name and she opened her eyes slowly and looked as if she was staring straight through me when I asked her if she was okay, although it was clear that she wasn't she then answered a sharp no, and continued talking more to herself than to me saying that too much of them were outside as a result of which she wasn't going back out there to listen to all that noise and she cannot understand their conversations because they don't make any sense to her.

I asked her when was the last time she took her meds, she just sprang up out of the chair, pushed me aside out of the way, walked-on inside and slammed the door. I was startled wondering if she had missed her meds or is it that her condition is getting worse or was she even taking her medication at all.

I would have Phillip check on her meds, but when I turned the handle of the door I found out that it wasn't locked then I saw her lying on her back with both hands behind her head as a pillow and she was staring up at the roof and talking to herself quietly. I walked out of the room and was just in time to see that the few people who were still there were all getting ready to leave, so I explained that Celia was exhausted and she wants me to tell them that she was happy and that they all made the day an enjoyable one. Her closest friend promised to call and check on her the next day.

I had told your father to check on Celia's medication, and when Carter and I were finished we had to check on her too. Phillip was just getting you into your PJ and Celia was out on the porch again this time standing there leaning forward with her hands on the rail, Phillip then told us that he had asked her about her meds, and she didn't answer him either but as far as he can tell it seems to him that she is still taking them. He then went into your nursery to put you to bed, so Carter and I went outside and joined Celia on the porch. We sat down in the chairs closest to her, but she kept standing there looking out into the back yard.

I started recapping the fun moments, how it was a great day for the outside activities and how I was most fond of the pictures which she had taken of you.

I was finding the day humorous but your mother wasn't having it, so when we saw that she still hasn't responded Carter went up to her and put his hand over hers, but she flinched so fast as if she was touched by a high voltage. He was startled, but remained calm and instead asked her if she was hungry or tired or if she feels she needs to talk, seconds which felt longer than what it was went by, but she finally answered and said that she was okay stating that she just needed some time by herself. We left her and went inside, and while we were about to leave Phillip entered the room informing us that he needed to take a shower and an early bed too, he was exhausted but before leaving I had him promise to call us if he needed to.

Your grandpa offered to stay with Celia if she wasn't ready for bed and so he did, he later called to inform us that Celia was asleep and he has seen to it that she took her medication before she went to bed. I didn't sleep well that night, so the following morning when I was on my way to her apartment, I saw Phillip on the other end coming over to see if Celia was with us, and when I told him she wasn't he became very anxious and headed outside looking for her a few minutes. He later returned without finding her although she wasn't scheduled for work until later that evening. Her car was still there so we were thinking that she couldn't have gone to see any of her friends since it was just about nine minute walk down the block.

I decided to give her a call with high hopes that your mom would be there but I got her voice mail in return, so your dad decided to go to the nearby park to look around, while Carter was with you in the kitchen preparing your breakfast.

When Kerry returned my call she was frightened to learn that we can't find your mom because she hadn't seen her also, but assured us that she will give us a call if she does stop by, she also asked us to keep her informed if anything came up.

Phillip called to let us know that she wasn't at the park either, but he was going to drive around and scout out the entire area, after about twenty minutes and still no sign of her we were getting really worried because it was chilly outside. I could remember the PJs she went to bed in because the night before when Phillip informed me that she was sleeping, I went over and checked on her and saw that it was a fleece pajama suit, so it was then I confirmed that she didn't leave in any other clothing aside one of her coats and her handbag, at least she was warm and her phone was by her bed.

She had left the house only God knows when because your father only found out that she wasn't there when he woke up to get ready for work, so the situation was becoming very tensed up with every minute that went by. It has been two hours since she was missing when Claudette reached the house, but in the meantime Celia's friend from church, Jean, was with Phillip on the road checking stores, and Carter was out there driving around too while Claudette and I stayed back at the house in the event that she turns up or to answer the phone if it should ring with any information of her.

While we were there waiting, I called our Reverend and he prayed with us for her safe return. It was about four hours after her disappearance that the house phone rang and I knew it had to be some news about her because that phone hardly rings. So, I grabbed it quickly with tension in my hands and in my voice, then I answered and when I heard the person on the other end identifying herself as the hospital that she usually works in, I felt a huge sense of relieve, although it was a brief conversation and I think I held my breath the entire time she was talking.

Celia was there as I was informed that she turned up that morning, she was supposed to work but the security saw how exhausted she was and then informed the doctors and they rushed her into ER. She was dehydrated because they were very sure that she had walked the entire journey there, they also noticed that she was still wearing her pajamas. They also informed me that they had already called her husband and he was on his way there, and she is still under the doctor's supervision, but by the time I hung up the phone there were missed calls from Carter, Phillip and Jean, So, we all decided to meet at the hospital while Claudette would stay with you.

Before I left the house I decided to call Jamaica in order to inform her mother about what was happening, after which we both cried and when I hung up she was still crying; this was so heavy on her. We had kept the early signs away from her because Celia didn't want her worrying and also the doctor said possibilities are that she could get better, but now we have to face the elephant in the room because there is no denying that Celia is sick so we can't keep it away from her, she is her daughter. I had sum it up for her and promised to keep her informed, and if it calls for her to travel down to come see her then we will make the arrangements.

I then made a call to her doctor and he advised us to bring her to see him when she got released from the hospital. Before I left for the hospital, Kerry arrived at the house with her two children ages two and five which got you so excited, and immediately all three of you started to play.

Arriving at the hospital she was already awake although she wasn't really looking like her regular cheerful self, but she managed to smile when I walked into her room. Your father had already filled her in although I don't know how she had taken it, but her first word to me was how is her baby girl doing, then I assured that apart from missing her mommy you were doing very fine and that I left you playing with Kerry kids. She brightened up when I told her that you even allowed the smaller one to keep your favorite stuff rabbit then she smiled and said a 'gentle heart as her mommy'. We all laughed out loudly, which helped to release the tension and gloom in the room.

For the rest of the visit, we talked about everything except on what had happened and all this time Phillip was sitting close to her caressing her and comforting her because the hospital was going to keep her overnight for observation. Phillip and Carter hadn't eaten because of such a hectic morning, so I forced them to leave and go get something to eat or to go stretch their legs, Jean stayed back a little while longer so as to help me freshen her up with her toiletries which I had brought from home and comb her hair during which time she was giving her words of encouragement, and how she should gather her strength so that she can go home to her family, and she should also know how much she was loved and we are all there to support her. I could see that she began to relax as her eyes looked so weak, but she was putting her best out because she do believe that she had family and friends who cares so much for her, she then told us that she was frightened when she woke up and saw Phillip at her bedside and she didn't fully understand what had happened as he had explained most of what he thinks he knows although she couldn't recall any of it, but she was glad that she ended up at the right place. Jean left shortly afterwards and promised to call and check on her.

By the time your father and Carter had returned, she was already in a better mood and when we reached the house that evening Kerry had already left and Claudette had prepared dinner, so we all ate and reflected on the day's event. We were still up when Phillip returned home from the hospital and broke the sad news to us.

We weren't surprised because we realized that she wouldn't be having a job any more at the hospital, the reality is that she is sick the doctors diagnosed her after thorough medical and concluded that she wasn't fit for that working environment, it was devastating being in that field and she too understood that it was the right thing to do, but hearing it that moment was too she had taken it hard on her.

Your father stayed with her while she cried, but it feels way better to have his support and she had wanted to come home, but they advised that it's best to have her there for at least twenty four hours while stating that they will release her the following day, and Phillip was to go by for her. Your mommy and your father reached the house that evening right before dinner, she seemed very weak which I guessed was from the medication, but she was in a cheerful mood for you and right away you started telling her about the activities you and Kerry children had done, she was asking questions and you kept chatting away as you were so happy and that kept her smiling at the dinner table as things seemed normal. We were all happy now that she was home, so the conversation was light and later in the family room the atmosphere was the same as all eyes were on you while you were laughing and playing running from your father to your mother.

He was tickling you while she was enjoying how happy you were and that alone makes all the difference. I was taking a few pictures but my favorite was when your father had you on the ground, you were laughing so hard that you called on your mommy to come get you but instead he caught her and started to tickle her too, you were all on the floor dying with laughter. Claudette stayed for a few days and she also accompanied me and Carter with Celia to her doctor for a routine check and for him to review the medication that the hospital had put her on, he further suggested various groups and programs to help her to cope with the transition. After leaving the doctor's office, Claudette went home and we returned to the house. Your dad had just finished fitting a toy play kitchen that your grandma Claudette had brought for you with the plastic food in shapes and colors of real food and plastic utensils; pots, cups and plates. You were excited to be able to prepare food, and so for the next couple of months all of us had to be joining you in your kitchen where you're always eager to serve us something.

Your father was leaving for work, so we all quietly left the room so that your mommy could get to spend those special moments with you, as she had joined you on the floor.

Days became weeks and reality was sinking in as she had become unemployed because of her illness. We were all there for her from time to time and most times she would get visits from Claudette, her friends and some others from church. She was dealing with the changes and learning to adjust, she tried to do everything just the same except going to work as she had sent in her resignation letter as advised by the hospital board.

We tried as much as we could not to leave her by herself for long especially with you, and wherever or whatever it is that she needed to get done on the road someone would go with her, or for instance to go to places like the park, the mall, or church until the doctor said otherwise. Celia who was well known for her social nature became so quiet now, but she didn't object to us being in her space and continual checking up on her. She had also joined in a social group, as we didn't want her to end up with any form of depression and she was also active in our church which played a great part in keeping her active. She was later appointed to be the youth choir director, young people meetup and coaching, this exposure helped so much in her healing process Their annual convention was fast approaching and the Reverend asked her to assist in having the youth ministry ready, she was excited to have them sing one of her original songs and she herself got the opportunity to sing an original one that she had written. The convention was finally a success as all the effort and planning had paid off. It was live streamed and after a few days someone contacted the church stating that he was interested in meeting your mom. He wanted to set up on appointment to see if she was interested in recording her music, and so she accepted the information but after they met she asked for some time to think about it. Months had past and the medication seemed to be working pretty fine as she was seen handling her full routines; carrying you to school, parks and other play areas including play dates with her friend's children, she also visited the gym four times per week and took good care of you and your dad.

Chapter Five

A part of the working world

One evening when we were all in the family room, she said that she had applied for a part time job at a nursing home facility for the elders a few months back, and she had received an answer of acceptance from them while also stating that it was the second time they had contacted her, but the reason she didn't say anything before or accept the job was because they wanted her to work full time. She had requested the afternoon shift so that she could carry you to school and pick you up before she went to work. She explained that this was something that she really wanted to do, and your dad said that they had talked about it and encouraged her before she went ahead to apply for the job. He had also informed us that he had suggested to her to try out the idea of getting her music recorded instead because she could choose how to use her time and it was more flexible, but she said that she wasn't feeling it. Her passion was to do what she loved so much and for now it's nursing, so we too encouraged her to go ahead and accept the job.

Your fourth birthday was in two weeks and she was in the process of planning your birthday party, so she decided to start her new job the week after it.

The party location was at "chick a cheese," the turnout was great and very exciting as you and the other children got to enjoy the activities there. You brought home lots of presents and we took pictures of you unwrapping for the next couple of days.

At the beginning of the new week as planned, your mother went back to work. It was about twenty minutes to and from work each day; she fitted in perfectly and really enjoyed it.

Celia would come back home when your grandpa and I was still up few nights, and so she would occasionally pop in to tell us goodnight. We were so happy to see her have her passion back as we could see that the fire was back in her eyes, she was basically doing well at her job and in her family life. Her mother had canceled her trip to come visit, but she and Celia were making proper arrangements for her, two of Celia siblings and us to go to Disney for your fifth birthday celebration, so Celia was determined to make this job workout for her. She had to save for this trip in order for her to have enough money to sponsor them. Phillip working schedule was during the days, so whenever he reached home from work he would take good care of you, get you ready for your bedtime so as to enable your grandpa and I get a break from an over-active four years old. You were always eager and happy whenever he reached home on most evening because he would always bring back something for you, and as a regular routine you both would always do something fun that he knows you would so much enjoy; like riding on his back or playing chef with you in your little kitchen or reading books.

You loved to read and sometimes you'll remember what you've learned or just read the pictures, and you had a couple of favorites, but animals and fairy princess books were mostly your books of choice as you would regularly want them to be read before you fall asleep.

But you and your mother's favorite pastimes was playing dress up because she loves nice clothes and that was also one of her traits that you have. She would dress you up in her accessories sometimes, you would even put your tiny feet in her flat shoes and as long as you can manage you would walk in them while she would either do a video or take pictures of you posing, and she usually does this on her days off from work because after all the dressing up you two would end up settling for one of those fashion to wear for the day. Your grandpa and I would see both of you coming over with these very weirdly or astounding fashion, at times we would want to die of laughter but we didn't dare do it in front of you, instead we lavish you with compliments and smiles which leads to both of you either ending up on the couch or in her bed watching princes movies. One morning she was to carry you to school and it was getting really late, but normally she would have packed your lunch and have you eat breakfast at the time.

I became worried, so I went over to find out what was happening then I found you in the sofa watching the television, so when I asked you where your mom was you pointed in the direction of her bedroom. I went in and there were clothes everywhere; on her bed or the floor, she was ranting but looking confused, the moment she saw that I had entered the room she stopped and just stood there looking at me blankly and when I asked her what was going on, she told me she was leaving with you. I gently asked her where was she going and she told me she was going home, I got confused and asked her where exactly was that because this was her home, she angrily shouted "no" so I then sought to know from her if she had a fight with your father, but again she snapped at me and said that she needed rest stating that she was tired. All this time, she was looking beneath the bed and searching the closet but couldn't find whatever she was looking for, so I wanted to know what she was looking for so I could assist her in finding it and again she snapped asking me how can she leave if she can't find the suitcase to pack both of your stuff. I was a little bit puzzled because she knew that the suitcases were stored in the storage room at the back of the garage, so I asked her when and where were the last place she saw any of the suitcases then her mood shifted and she began to think. She tilted her head and looked so focused, but she couldn't remember where the suitcases were normally kept, instantly a depressing feeling just flooded me and all my limbs became weak. I said to myself 'dear God she is getting sick again'. She was still thinking at least she was calm which was actually what I wanted, so in order to distract her I kept telling her that I can assist in finding them, and if unfortunately we don't find any in the house we can go to the mall and buy some, but first we need to pack away the clothes into the drawers until we get the suitcases because the place looks too untidy and she won't be able to sort or find the stuff easily when she is ready to pack them into the suitcases. Somehow she thought it was logics and she agreed and began to put them back into the drawer, then I volunteered to put your stuff into your room while she does hers.

When we had finished putting away the stuff I told her that Carter had made breakfast and we were all hungry especially you, so I went and collected you from in front of the TV and the three of us went to have breakfast that morning. Your grandpa had made pancakes eggs and oatmeal which was everyone's favorite; he had already eaten and left for the store to run some errands. Your mommy wasn't talking but at least she was calm and she was eating. Soon after finishing our breakfast, we were still sitting around the table and then I handed her the medication and made sure she took them, at the time it was too late to take you to school.

I had called her doctor and we set an appointment for that afternoon and all three of us went to his office. He didoes his regular check but his main issues was that she stayed on her meds and take them on specific time then he went on to explain that there is a lot of different behaviors associated with her illness, but my complain to him was that despite the fact that she was still on medication, she sometimes dissociate herself from others whom she knows very well in a way as if she doesn't recognize them or even her surroundings. She would even loss track of time and or what she was doing, talk to herself or some imaginary person, but my main concern was if her condition will get worse and how long will she be like that, none of which he could positively answer. His main advice was to keep her on the medication and she should stick with the specific time in taking them, get as much rest as possible, and try to stay away from stressful situation, he then referred us again to support group or and be a member. Celia has checked out a few before and loves two of them, but so far she still hasn't joined and he was adamant to know why she hasn't because they have experience and answer to question that we her family members doesn't know. He strongly recommended that she would be a part of some well establish people who can relate and get her the right kind of support.

After the doctor's office, we stopped by at a restaurant to eat Buffalo wings and burger; her second favorite food apart from her Jamaican dishes, but on rare occasions she would enjoy Indian dishes or tacos. We stayed at the restaurant to have lunch, but before we could finish our meal she started to sweat. By the time I could figure out what was going on, she sprang from the table with her hands over her mouth rushing to the restroom, so I went after her with you in my arms.

She was inside there barfing, so by the time she was finished and we left the ladies room her skin was pale and her eyes looked weak. I was thinking that she might be pregnant, so I asked her about it and her reply was that she didn't know, but it could be possible. I was in disbelief because I wondered why she would want to do that to herself and her family knowing well that she isn't capable of raising two children in her present state. If it wasn't for her illness without a doubt she could, but her condition is unpredictable. Phillip has said he didn't want another child and Carter and I are going up in age, so helping her raise another child we could do but supposedly anything happens to her, I didn't see us raising kids by ourselves which was a huge concern to me.

She too seemed unraveled by the thought of it. Was there something going on that I wasn't aware of, did Phillip change his mind about wanting another child? Celia had lost her appetite and we didn't eat much so the waiter helped pack our food to go, she also picked up dinner for your father; a beef burger lover. After leaving the restaurant, she also stopped by the pharmacy and bought a pregnancy test kit, when I tried to talk to her more about it on our way home she changed the subject because she didn't want to talk about it, so I let it go until we confirm for certain what was actually going on.

As for your father you could see he is trying his best to hold it together and I do admire him for that because it wasn't easy, there is a lot going on for him to handle as he got scared and almost messed up his family, but he still stayed and they worked it out.

He loves your mommy and he adores you. Celia's condition looked daunting but everyone tried to support them both, your dad also got closer to Carter and after they had the talk he had seemed to trust and respect him. They were so close that they spent more time with each other rather than just watching sports at home and doing grill; they started going places together.

Most times when he was going to the park with you he would ask your grandpa to tag along, they also went shopping to the men's store and the hardware store, they visited sport bar to have a drink and watch the game, and most importantly go bowling, it was a favorite for your grandpa, but he rarely ever go there anymore.

I guess he told Phillip and it was fun to give him that treat by following him there. I was glad the way your father had affected Carter's life too, he had retired a while back, he was content and happy with his life, and his family's life, but now spending time with your dad and going places outside of the regular was so much lovable to him. He was more relaxed and anyone could see that he was enjoying it, he even started visiting the gym more often than once per week which he had been doing for years. And on the other side personally, Carter's support was having a positive impact on your father and it was very encouraging to see how close they had become.

I was still in my thoughts on how another baby might be a stretch; everything was just too complex at the moment to go down that road, I sighed. Just then Celia parked into the driveway put her hand on my shoulder and told me to stop worrying because it clearly showed in my face. It was soon time for her to leave for work so she went to get ready, so she took you with her to your room for a nap.

It was about two hours later when you both returned, she kissed and tickled you a little and then placed you on the sofa. She came over to hug me and whispered that I should remember what she had said earlier that I need not worry, she smiled and I hugged her back, as I watched her drive off to work, I finally released that pent up energy by letting lose my shoulder and let my arms drop and just took some deep breaths.

The morning had started out crazy and frightening, but things took a turn and she had become calm and collective and became herself once again. I said a silent prayer that she will be okay, I then went over and sat on the couch beside you completely unaware of anything except your focus on the TV screen, but Carter wasn't because he wants to know what was going on, so I briefed him on the entire morning happenings and also that it's a possibility that Celia might be pregnant, so he got upset which he rarely does. He then told me that there was something going on with your dad, I wasn't totally surprised though but I told him it's obvious that he seemed to know something that we don't which caused him to get angry on hearing that Celia might have another baby, and was I in for a bigger surprise as there was no way I was prepared for what I heard next?

Phillip had been having an affair with an ex-girlfriend from Canada, and whenever he went there it was to be with her whereas it was about a year since he had officially ended the relationship with her. He was cheating on Celia for three years of their marriage, and the last time he had moved out it was because she was pressuring him to leave your mother and move up to Canada to live with her. He had told her that there is no way he's going to leave his daughter, but she told him to bring you along with him while clearly informing him that she would not continue to see him if he doesn't leave your mommy.

They weren't friends when he met Celia, as she was married to someone else but it didn't work out so she started to confide in Phillip and he also told her about Celia's illness, and at the time she had filed for divorce from her husband which gave them a go ahead to start seeing each other again. I couldn't believe my ears that after all this time he was running out on Celia he was actually going into someone else arms, and she was always blaming herself thinking that she was the problem and the reason why he feels trapped and unhappy, but she was feeling it too and suffering with guilt when all this time her selfish husband was thinking only of himself. The more I thought about it the angrier I got, and why tell Carter and why now? There were so many questions floating around in my head. When I said all that to him he got out of the recliner and come over and sat down closer to me, again I asked him why Phillip told him of the affair, and was it truly over? He answered in almost a whispering tone 'because there was a baby involved'. I suddenly felt a heavy gloom over me, my stomach became tightened as I was trying to catch my breath. I was trying to focus on what he had just told me, but it was blurry. I was also lost of words and he became so worried too because of the strokes I suffered after the tragedy of our son, he then stopped. I asked him for a glass of water and when he returned, I told him that I was fine and he should continue.

I learnt that they had a baby boy together and he will be two in a couple of months, the mother still lives in Canada and she had brought the baby to visit Phillip four times and he had went to visit his son two times in the past, and of course his mother knew about it and she also get to see her grandson at will.

When Carter had finished talking I was bewildered, what the hell was going on all these secret, what was going to happen when Celia finds out it has being less than a month since Carter knew about it? He had figured it out by spending time with Phillip, and he had confronted him and asked him what he was hiding and so he revealed everything.

It became clear what was actually happening, Phillip put Carter and I into a messy situation that he had created, how did Carter not see that coming and now I got pulled into it.

I became really upset because his stupid behavior caused him to be in this situation. Whatever it is he is going through, he needs to figure out what type of relationship he really wants and if he even wants it at all.

Phillip had seen that Carter was in that father figure space and he abused that trust by unloading his secrets that he has being hiding from our daughter, how callous of him and now everyone knows about it except Celia. She will be devastated when she finds out, worst yet this could tip her off the far end, their marriage, and their child.

Carter made it clear that Ashia could lose any one or even both parents, but to keep this away from her by living a life of lies knowing of her husband infidelity is going to be tragic either ways and this was pressuring for us. The thing is that we don't know how she would take it, she could end up hating us for telling her or for keeping it from her if she finds out later, and that we know all along.

As for Phillip, his guilt has being bugging him although he told your grandpa that he was willing to live with it a secret from your mother as long as it takes and he has no intentions of separating his family. I find that very hard to believe and I made it clear to Carter that Phillip was being pressured and didn't know how best to deal with it and wants someone else to do his dirty works and watch to see how it would unfolds. Then I remembered the pregnancy test kit that she had picked up earlier and my heart sunk. What if she was with child in a marriage in which they are living in a lie and in shambles? It seemed as though whatever forward move they had made was only to have put them two steps back at that moment.

I could only pray that she wasn't pregnant, and even if she was then it could have happened a few weeks back when they went to Cancun, Mexico, to celebrate their fifth anniversary. It was only for the weekend, but from Celia's excitement they had a wonderful and lovely experience.

Claudette had suggested that she would have kept you for the three days that your parents would be away which was very considerate of her while explaining that your grandpa and I could use the rest. Fact of the matter still remained that since both your parents were working we were babysitting you full time, which was fine with us because first you were an adorable child, so sweet and smart but you were very energetic during the times we had to take care of you, as there was your mother, your father and the time you're at school, but we appreciate your grandma's offer to keep you. We did stay at home for those days but you were missing, the house was so quiet.

Celia sent us pictures and videos of some of the fun she was having during their vacation, as it was a total success. They returned late that Sunday evening and we didn't see them until the following morning.

She didn't bring you to school, Claudette did but she would be the one to pick you up that afternoon before she went to work, and so for a couple of hours that morning we talked about her trip, how she was happy that they did go on that vacation because they were relaxed and focused only on enjoying each other's company. Spending the few days she felt the positive shift in their energy and she knew without a doubt that they were still in love. She expressed how confident she was that their relationship will be stronger and better, she also stated that the hotel they stayed played a factor in it as they felt like honeymooners because the atmosphere created that ambiance of pleasure and intimacy. They had also participated in couple's group games, one that has been a quiz about how much you know or understand your partner, and another one is memories and places.

She had returned home with a determined mindset to make her marriage work, to fight for her family and start living in gratefulness and stop living in fear, and also stop letting worry hold her in hostage instead she will be learning how to have better communication with her husband and also focus her awareness on being a better mother and wife in her relationship. She had really said a lot that day and I could see she finally realized that what is needed to be successful in their relationship is to have progressive growth and for that to happen the work has to be done. She even listened as I told her about the struggle your grandfather and I had being through, they are found in every marriage or relationship but they should be accepted because there only a test, and each time you pass it strengthens your union to balance. This out make wonderful moments are critical in the survival of any relationship to work and there is no avoiding it, the good times and the bad times are real.

But mostly appreciating what God had blessed her with because it was more than what she dreamt of. She was going to make the best of what is available by living in the moment and be happy in the present. I was totally tuned in to her while listening, I was certain that she was clear on what she wants and positive about the direction on where her life would be heading.

She got real about her musical ambition and she began to recognize that it was her talent because it comes so natural to write and she had the voice to sing, but growing up she would dream of being a nurse so she usually looked at writing as a hobby, but the more she writes the more passionate she felt about music. She even expressed her feelings about it to your father while they were there on vacation, and he was very supportive and encouraging telling her that he knew all along, and as a matter of fact everyone saw it. She was basically the only one who didn't and this was a fact, but we all knew one day that she would realize it.

It was our Reverend that advised us to let her be because that day God got her ready to use her music to speak and reach out to souls, it's going to just happen. She was clear on it and she will be fine to make some adjustments, but first she is going to put a timeline on when and how to move forward with doing music full time. Just looking at her I knew she was going to be transforming, she had found that her calling would make her life experience more fulfilling than ever because she had clarity now.

Would hearing this news create a setback? What effect would it cause I looked over at you playing with your toys on the floor without having the least idea of what was going on; with this happening will it to disrupt the only life you have known the surroundings the family there is no telling the damage that this secret could cause.

Chapter Six

His secret is out

When Phillip left the house that evening, I couldn't help from not confronting him because I was beyond angry; I was furious. He could only listen while I did vent because this was the very first time he had seen me this angry, and as a matter of fact it was the first time in a long time that I was this angry.

When he finally got the chance to respond to me, his explanation was the same as he had told Carter, stating that it was a secret and he had a plan to keep it away from your mother as long as he could. He continued to say that he knew there wasn't an excuse for what he had done, and that it wasn't his intention for her and the rest of the family to find out.

I then got sarcastic with him about a neat way of putting it, since he had the gut of telling Carter his intentions which was to be kept a secret, knowing well where that would lead. He went on to state that all he could think about is your mother's health and he would never forgive himself if his action should cause an irreparable damage to his wife and the mother of his child, and that is the price he was willing to pay. He had not intended for us to know that he had that burden to keep a secret or to deceive Celia because he had being living with this guilt for over two years and it was eating at him deeply. He didn't know what came over him that night he told Carter, but it wasn't for a reason to cause trouble, he kept apologizing.

I made him know that it doesn't even matter when Celia finds out the fact that he had a child which he needs to be a father to, and his wife needs to know about it. I could see that he was torn up about it as he was hurting at that moment. I could feel nothing but empathy for him, but in the same instance knowing that my daughter didn't ask for this and no matter what, his hurt couldn't compare to hers.

Three days later, we were in our Reverend's office, he had made arrangements for us to see him. After finding out about your dad other baby, I couldn't think straight. I was stressed out and your mother saw it and asked me what was going on, but before I could tell her something like I'm tired or any other excuses of a lie, she said I know what's going on. I was a bit startled that I started wondering how she could have known, did Phillip tell her? She didn't pick up on my sudden change because she continued talking, she said "mom stop worrying, I'm not pregnant." She told me that she did the test that previous day after she had returned home from work, while assuring me that she was going to be okay. So in my own view, the secret has to end.

I know something needs to be done and it should be as early as possible, we were bumping heads until Carter decided to have us call him. After briefly explaining what was going on he agreed to meet with Phillip, Carter and I so we set the time to meet with him when we knew Celia would be at work, so she wouldn't suspect anything that day. I saw Phillip crying, it was heartfelt as he had to be released.

It took me back to the day when I really witnessed Carter crying and it had been seven months after the death of our son on a Tuesday morning. I could clearly remember because it was the day after his birthday although it was a wonderful day outside but it didn't feel that way. We had decided to clear out their apartment, the two bedrooms, the living rooms and everything that was theirs, and after the movers had left, I couldn't find Carter. I had expected that he was still in there but when I found him, he was sitting on the couch with tears flowing down his face.

I could only go over and hug him while he rested his head on me with his body was trembling, he needed that release. He finally could let it go and so that day I did the same for your dad. But the meeting was worth it as the Reverend had come up with a great plan that we all agreed on, which could at least help to alleviate the pain when your mother finally knows. He had suggested to be their relationship coach for at least three months on every areas of their relationship before your father told her about your brother.

The Reverend knows these things usually break up a relationship, but during these sessions they can test the love they have for each other and the strength of their relationship to see if it's worth fighting for, and so for the next three months once per week for an hour they, stick to the appointment. Celia had already had that mindset after returning from their anniversary vacation to do whatever it takes to keep her family together, so that day when your father suggested they should consider couples coaching with their Reverend, she was happy to see that Phillip wants to be involved to make their marriage work. She continues to attend the support group once per week, and interesting enough she started to focus more on her writing. She was having an impact on her solos; she sings in church and whenever she writes for the choir they always loved it, at that time she still hasn't contacted the person who wants to work with her on her music.

One Sunday after she finished singing one of her songs that brought almost the entire congregation to tears, the Revenant told the church that your mother had a story to tell the world and he knows her talent is writing, he said a time will come when she will be putting her music out there to bless hearts, save souls and change minds with. The months flew by as they continued to meet with the Reverend, she told me it was worth it and sometimes she would brief me on their progress. They also applied what he had instructed them to do outside of their regular routine.

They both understood that the strategy he was giving them was an opportunity for them to see their relationship worth, to acknowledge areas that they needed to focus on, and clarity on how to be consistent in proving their love for each other.

We all know that she is going to flip when she heard about her husband's infidelity and the fact that it also brought forth a child. He was preparing her for what next; what would really be her ultimate decision after finding this out?

We all knew the day your father had a plan on telling her about it, they went out for a romantic dinner that weekend because it was his birthday, and she had arranged everything for that Saturday evening.

She made the reservation at a five-star Italian restaurant, a candlelight dinner on the terrace overlooking the city, she wore an elegant dress that compliments her body with matching heels and clutch bags and diamond earrings. She was gorgeous I must say, there are pictures of this evening in your collection. The evening had turned out great because that Sunday morning before we left for church your mother couldn't stop talking about it. Phillip, on the other hand, was trying to be involved but was mindfully occupied that following day in their session with Reverend because that's the time he is going to tell her.

They went that Monday afternoon for their session, for all who knew it was tense, as we didn't know what to expect, only Celia thought it was business as usual. It went somewhat civilized but given the circumstances, it was as expected, it happened at the church and with the Reverend.

She had stated that she wants nothing to do with him, she didn't want to be around him and she wanted him out of the house.;;;;;; kind of what was expected, he left her at the office with Reverend, went home and packed some of his stuff and moved in temporarily with his mother.

That day when she finally reached the house your father had already left, but he had written to her a letter apologizing again, acknowledging that he will respect her space but he would be visiting his daughter until your mother decided what she is going to do. When I approached her to talk she made it clear that she didn't want to talk about it because everyone except her had already known and Reverend had already filled her in on everything.

Instead she left to pick you up from school and it took her a longer time to return home. So, I called her to know how she was doing but she sounded upset while telling me that you guys went to lunch and she took you to the park. When she arrived at the house later that day she went straight to her apartment, we realized that she wasn't coming over for dinner, so Carter took some food to her, and when he returned he told me that you and your mom was curled up on the couch watching some kids program, he tried to talk to her but she wasn't in the mood for it. For the next couple of days the atmosphere was tense, still Celia wasn't talking to anyone but she was home. I guessed that she might have requested some time off from work, she was very calm and we gave her the space she needed. Phillip made arrangements with her on the days he wants to spend time with you so he would take you to his mother's house, and he also collected more of his clothes. She would leave the house whenever he is coming by and ask me to let her know when he had left.

She didn't take her wedding band off or say anything about a divorce which was a good sign, but for the next session she told him she wouldn't want him there, he agreed and she went by herself.

It was the third Sunday since they last being together at church and he comes by the house for you, I asked him to stay for dinner we were all at the table your mom included she told him that she would love to have him moved back into the house but she decided to have them hired a couples coach to move forward.

Two months later we all get to meet Phillip's son, Celia requested that you get to meet your brother so your dad booked a weekend trip for him and his mother to visit and they would have stayed at Claudette's house so the first day he bring him by our house, you didn't understand much but you get the idea that you're close, and for the three days he came by the house the two of you would play and bond together.

Your mother being who she was couldn't help but be a part of this moment because she was so fond of children.

I think this was good for everyone we no longer look at Phillip son as an outsider, most importantly Celia doesn't look on him as a mistake to his husband infidelity, but a child who needs his father to be a part of his life, she sees him as no longer a threat or a stranger but as a blessing, this is what the essence of life is all about, she had gathered some peace from this experience, her mood was different more pleasant, her vibe has shifted.

It was coming on to your fifth birthday and as plan they will be celebrating it at Disney, it was for four days and Celia's mother and two of her smaller sister will meet them there and spend an additional six more weeks at my house before returning home.

Your father had implied that it would be a good idea to have his son on the trip, which Celia shut down instantly, she was even infuriated at him to even have suggested it in the first place she had been planning the trip for a year now to have him change it, definitely not, she wants it to be memorable with pictures and videos as it was your first Disney trip.

The communication didn't go well and it was their first major disagreement, Phillip said, he didn't understand why your mother would object to his idea because she now knows about his son and had accepted him.

His reasoning was getting the chance to spend time with his son will be scares. She was still against it but suggest that when his son is at least five years old when he can be a part of their family vacation without his mother then she will be prepared for that which she thought was a good way of compromising that issue, but Phillip had other plans

They leave the Thursday to return home that Sunday but that Friday afternoon when we were on the phone I could tell something was wrong, when I asked her about it she was a little hesitant but too upset to keep it all in, she blurted it out she was cursing and crying I couldn't get clear on what she was saying but from what I heard I know what was going on so I listen, after a few minutes and she had finally release all her pent up anger I ask her where you were, she told me you were with her mother and sisters you were at lunch but she was too upset to eat.

She told me that she hasn't the least idea that Phillip baby mother and his son were going to be there, it was that same morning that he told her that they were there.

His explanation was that he had mentioned the trip to his sons mother, she indicates that it would be a wonderful idea if his son was there and she doesn't think it would cause a problem for anyone seems as it is a public place, he had agreed with her thinking that Celia wouldn't have a problem with them being there at Disney, so when your mother disagree he couldn't go back on his promise and there is no way he could get Celia to change her mind, it would only lead to another argument so he leave it hoping that she would understand and accept it.

A couple of hours has passed since he left with her and their son he had asked her if their daughter could go with him but she told him no, so she was basically going to make the most of the trip as enjoyable as possible for your sake her mother and sisters, which she make happen she continued to send me pictures and we talk over the next few days. When you all return home your grandma and aunts stay in my guest room your mother didn't want her to worry about what was going on with her and Phillip so she hid things from her.

Older folks are keen on details she asked me to explain to her what was happening with your parents and their relationship, I didn't say much because as much as she is my sister Celia is still her daughter and it's up to her to tell her mother what she wants her to know, however she knows about his outside child and the fact that they were there at Disney so we talk about that, also explaining to her that they showing up was a last minute decision. During their stay your mother goes all out to make them happy so they have a fun time visiting huge malls historical sites amusement parks and a lot of shopping so she was really busy after Disney, to focus much on her own life.

The day your grandma were leaving Celia gave her a photo album she had created of her family but most of those pictures was about you, your grandma was so excited I think it will be the most cherish gift she had receive from Celia.

As the days becomes weeks it seems your mother had more and more gloomy days I brought it to Phillip attention, he said he also noticed it but he wasn't too concern because he was monitoring her medication and as far as he can tell she is up to date on them he tried to get her to talk, but she said she was writing more and with everything else in her day to day activities she was just exhausted, he said he had also bring it up in one of their sessions but her answer was the same, and he remind me that her doctors had said there will be days like these her sickness and or medication could trigger moods.

We decided to monitor her closely and it continued like she wasn't going to break out of that sequence anytime soon, but one lovely day while our landscape was being done and Carter as usual was outside holding a conversation, I brought out lemonade so I sat there on the patio watching them shortly after Celia join me so we were enjoying the cool breeze and sunshine and laughing and chatting, I was happy to see that this was one of her good days but during our conversation I notice oftentimes she strayed completely from the topic, and that wasn't my real concern it was the fact that she didn't even realize it, she would have continued talking sometimes not making sense to me because I couldn't understand what event she was speaking of or who she was talking about and I was there listening to her just skip from one conversation to the middle of something else, until Carter join us on the patio.

She was getting things done as usual but most days as if she was going through the motions it looks as if she was falling into a state of depression then automatically just snap out of it and she would be happy and involved with whatever was happening around her.

Later we find out that she stop going to the support group and then the couples session with your father she was still giving excuses but it was obvious that she rather be anywhere except at these sessions, worst she wasn't telling him why she lost interest but your father had been getting impatient after he showed up at their third sessions alone, he was also losing money so he confront her about it and it becomes boisterous.

Carter and I was in the kitchen when we heard something like a shouting match completely startled it didn't resonate at first unaware of what was going on and where it was coming from that noise had never happened in our home before.

Carter and I rushed over to find you looking at them and crying and both of them shouting at each other on the top of their voice, so I just went over and pick you up and carry you away from that scene, leaving Carter to intervene.

I brought you over to our kitchen and serve you some ice cream it works, right away you stop crying and was enjoying your treat about half an hour later when Carter join us we were sitting on the couch watching cartoons on the television, we didn't want to talk about what had just happen in front of you, but he only told me that Phillip had left saying he will be back soon and your mother was getting ready for work, he then leave for the kitchen to finish preparing dinner and I just stayed with you observing how absorb you were into the cartoon, less than an hour later she rush in apologizing, she then pick you up start kissing you and telling you how much she loved you and rush out through the door for work.

By the time Phillip had return you were fast asleep so he just collect you said goodnight and head over to their apartment to put you to bed later Carter told me he got Phillip to walk with him outside that's the only way he could get them to stop and the only thing he said is that your mother is accusing him of still having an affair with his sons mother, he denied it and she gets angrier so she basically told him she was wasting her time going to these sessions about their relationship when he has another relationship going on.

She didn't say anything to me, but for certain she wasn't going to either sessions another two weeks blow off, and they were back at it again luckily this time you were at school Carter and I intervene again this time we get them to stop arguing so we can at least find out what the cause or what was happening, Celia did had a lot to say her believes is that since his husband secret is out he had assume that he can make a public display by putting it in her face and she should just accept it and also go along with it, your father was shaking his head from side to side and saying no but your mother seeing him she continues to explain why it was so, most instances where his son mother was on the phone he would prolonging the conversation as if they were best buddies talking about the games, it was really uncomfortable for her in the room she talk to him about how she felt explaining that she would rather they plan a time when she isn't around, but if she is and it's not an emergency let her know that he will call her back.

In your father defense he was not going to talk in private because has nothing to hide from Celia he was showing her that she should trust him, in the meantime Celia was explaining that he wasn't listening to her request and this is the reason why he is triggering her, she keeps telling him how she feels when he was on the phone with his ex for a lengthy conversation which seems unnecessary, but at times she happens to walk in on them unexpected and he usually gets off the phone right away so she started to make boundaries and one of them is that she won't go to any more of their relationship sessions with him, when he's not even listening to her.

What causes another fight that morning was still her husband lack of respect they both were in the kitchen fixing breakfast when his phone rung because it was closer to her, she look at it and see that it was his child mother so she answer it and told her he would return her call, his ex was upset asking her why did she answer Phillip phone and where he was she need to talk to him right away so Celia told her to go ahead and talk the phone is on speaker he is right there he will hear.

At that moment Phillip try to snatch the phone from her and she hung up the call, he got angry she was asking him explain to her what had just occurred over the phone why with his exs'-attitude but instead he got angrier that's how the shouting match begins.

We didn't know what was going on in there coaching sessions but that day listening to your mother she was really frustrated, she also think that her husband view on the whole situation that he had created was that he no longer had to bare his responsibility because it's out in the open, she needed to compromise and therapy is a place where your mother can vent what she was feeling so he put up with her during these session so he doesn't have to deal with it at home.

She continued by saying her husband wasn't the least concern with their relationship it feels as if she is carrying all the burden.

Chapter Seven

Who's to be hurt, who's to blame

Your father believe on what he is doing is enough he chooses to stay, he is paying for the sessions, he makes time to be available, he wants his wife and his daughter to be happy, but the reality of things is not the same and it will never be because his focus is not at one place anymore, his intentions for the sessions was to find some sort of common ground but it's not happening, he is trying to get things figured out too but in his defense, Celia is causing herself unnecessary stress why can't she see that there isn't anything personal between him and his son mother, he was saying he started to see her as being selfish because it has nothing to do with how she sees things and everything to do with how she wants them to be. I have to let him know that there is nothing wrong or selfish in someone wants it's for their own peace of mind or accomplishments it's considered personal, now how does the other person factors that how does it resonate will he make way or provide it or should it requires adjustments for the other person or does this causes frustration or ones peace of mind in no uncertain terms I told them for once, they really need to listen to what the other person is trying to say because there uncontrollable behavior will not happen again with or without my granddaughter around, so the need to deal with that issue once and for all, because more will arise soon and I will not allow you to grow in such an environment.

As for Phillip he needs to get a grip of things because what seems to be happening with him is he had one person talking in one ear and another person talking in the other ear and he needs to find a solution and quickly, because it's obvious what he thinks is working is definitely not.

By the time we were finished talking that morning it was time for you to get pick up from school I went with your mother and Carter stay with your dad because we see that the both of them need an intervention and that moment was it.

I briefly asked her to tell me about what the future holds for their daughter if this is how they are going to be living and so that day I get a better understanding of what was going on with her.

She told me, that from the beginning of their relationship it was a struggle for her, she had felt guilty that she didn't let him know before her pregnancy that she was schizophrenic, although without a doubt she know they were in love and Phillip express in so many ways that he needs her to be his wife, baby or not they would be married.

But the guilt she has been living with and fighting every day since he finds out about her schizophrenic, would he have still stayed if when he found out that she has a lifetime illness she wasn't expecting his child, did he feel that he was being tricked, does he sometimes felt resentment towards her, does he felt inadequate to settle with someone like her, she explained that she strongly believe he wouldn't stay and somehow she felt like she had trap him, she felt fake, there was always a mental battle going on in her head and so she tells herself that it was up to her to not let him regret marrying her.

She understood it takes work for any relationship to be successful, with this mindset she is putting a lot of pressure on herself with the responsibility to see to it that their relationship doesn't fail.

She felt the pain of his disrespectful behavior and it might be judged or come across to others as she being naive or lack of confidence, but the sacrifice she is willing to pay as no limits if she is going to make her daughter get the life she dream for her.

From her knowledge of his other child and the ex who is convincing him to return to her, she had been living in fear because she could see how easily your dad could get custody of you and worst he would be moving away to Canada, thinking about it causes her to be paralyzed in fear she couldn't bear the thought of losing you to the extent where she won't get to touch you or even to visit, so she tries harder to keep the relationship going with her main priority is to keep you safe, healthy and happy but when this got jeopardize, what next?, they can't even control themselves around you.

She had noticed when you were there to witness the previous fight and you were crying fear was in your eyes, she lost it more because she felt helpless, she sees everything crumbling around her so she became angrier she was shouting in the face of Phillip, but in fact she was shouting at her own life.

After returning home that night after work she didn't sleep not even for a minute she felt empty and lost sitting there in the dark her mind was flooded with thoughts she couldn't even tell if your father had realized she wasn't even in bed or he didn't care, but one thing for certain he hadn't once leave the bedroom to check if she was even in the house.

That morning when he went into the kitchen she had prepared breakfast he did apologize and he also ate before he left for work, but what was surprising for me that morning is understanding her resilience, with a new mindset she was saying that if it comes down to where she has to let Phillip get to raised you to prevent you from witnessing that kind of confrontation with the both of them ever again she would not fight it because never will she intentionally causes that fear in you again.

By this time we had reached your school and the moment you were in the vehicle she was a loving mom in a second wants to know how was your day happy and laughing when you start talking to her about what happened at school, to see that instant transformation of her, my thoughts were this is what an extraordinary mother looks like.

We had a stop at the store on our way back home we were pushing you in one of the shopping carts even these small things that put a smile on your face your mother would make a note.

You fell asleep on the ride home so I get the chance to talk to her giving her some advice on self-care on how she needs is to start placing more focus on herself, pay more attention on areas of her life that she needs to relax because she deserves it. I had also pointed out to her that the essential things in life was given to us freely she doesn't need to be fighting all the time, even soldiers get time out from fighting.

There is no way she can control every situation even trying to do so would burn her out the only thing that she can do is having a grateful heart and mind and a happy spirit by doing her best and let the future unfolds as is.

She had planned on making a special dinner that evening for you and your dad but when we reaches the house to find that your dad and grandpa had make a lovely dinner of rice and peas bake chicken corn and the cub cream potato and a vegetable salad, although she had prefer to prepare dinner chicken alfredo and enjoy a quiet evening, but we were pleased to see that the guys had out done themselves so we all enjoyed a delicious dinner and the company. Later that evening they bring you to the park so I figure that the talk that Celia and I have earlier and having Carter also talk with Phillip had turned out productive.

He had explained that what Phillip wanted was for Celia to trust him because he has nothing going on behind her back and he wasn't trying to hurt her when he talks to his son's mother in her presence or by wanting her to get involved but he wasn't listening that this is not what she wanted, as a matter of fact it was making her very uncomfortable.

His thoughts were that he had things under control, but she was still unforgiving and being nagging.

He didn't want to admit the burden he had put on her the strain he was causing her mentally emotionally and physically because in his mind he was the one who has a schizophrenic has a wife, the mother of his daughter that he has to deal with for the rest of life, his action was a form of being rebellious but he was truly sorry and he promises he won't cause her any more pain, Carter let him know he keep retracing his step what he needs to do is put into action what he says and just work on having a better communication experience with his wife and try to understand what she is going through too.

A few weeks later after dropping you off at school she come by the house she was so excited she had finally make an appointment to meet with the person who wants to produce her music she had always been visiting other branches of the church to sing and doing a few events she indeed got a collection of good songs that the world was waiting for.

That morning your dad accompany her to the studio to meet with the man who is interested in having her recording and producing her music, and the bonus is that he owned a radio station Michael has been in the business for over twenty years and he was impressed with her writing and her voice he promised her that without a doubt doing songs is her gift.

They spend the entire day in the studio, we pick you up from school and when they finally return home, Celia told us that she was resigning from nursing and take up her music as a profession.

Michael had told her that there was a lot to be done for her to take it to the next level and for now the demand was going to take a lot of her time.

She had agreed that this was the time for her to live her passion it was hard for her to quit her job she loves caring for others, being a nurse was very fulfilling for her but she has the support of family and friends, especially the church family through this transition. They were always nagging her to do her gospel music on a bigger platform some of her songs will need back-up singers and that is an area she also had to focus on to recruit some persons from the branches of the church to be a part of her team.

We all know that she would do good in her singing business because most of her songs was inspirational but to our surprise she did more that good, in less than a year she was getting extremely high airplay she had blown up social media, she had done quite a few interviews and she had to be choosing which events or concerts she could perform at, so her manager have to be turning away offer she was in demand but she was never going to forget that she was a wife and a mother first so her family was her top priority, a lot different from her regular nine to five jobs but you were never short of attention with your father, two grandmothers, your grandpa and even both your Godparents in your life.

The changes takes time, a process for everyone to adjust to but there was a transformation in your mother and father relationship, it was enlightening to see them around each other they certainly value each other's presence, happy spending time together they have finally reach that bliss in their relationship.

Your mother had her first album out less than two years into the business and was doing really well for herself and her family she has being on tour but didn't accept any international events so far.

One day after your father bring you home from school he said he had to talk to your grandpa and I, Celia had being away on a four days tour and he had received a call from her manager that she had to cancel some upcoming event, nothing of seriousness because those dates weren't near, but she had told her manager that she was tired, Karen had tried to talk her out of it but she seems to have made up her mind.

So she has reaches out to Phillip to have him talk to her, if it's even hold off a little longer to take some time to think about it because all she has at that moment is two single events in three weeks.

He was saying to us he understands why Karen would be a concern because the furthest booking was four months away and she had to cancel that too, so he need to let us know or if we could give him any advice as to what he should do, he would prefer if he could talk to her to get her to understand that she should take Karen's advice, she knows the music business and how it works.

We told him it's better to let it go and trust that she knows what she is doing, left her with whatever decision she makes, we are family our standpoint and Karen's are not the same it is her job, she is in it for the money, it's business as usual, yes she know about Celia sickness she is compassionate and very supportive with her, she even monitor her and her medication while she is away from home of course, but first she don't know Celia on a personal level what it is like for her and her feelings.

We intervene without she asking for it might cause her to be offended it would seem that we don't trust that she is capable of making her own decision, or being too hasty, either way that doesn't come off right she just might need him now as her husband, he needs to just be patient.

Secondly shouldn't we ignore the fact that she might be really tired, or having some side effects of her sickness the best we can do when she is back home is to give her the support she needs in the end he was satisfied with our conversation.

After she returns home she was sleeping longer and sometimes she had slight headache we thought she needs the rest she also visited her doctor he changes some of the medication but there was not much changes your dad said she would be up for hours at night but she would sleep in late so we allowed her to sleep, and fill in with helping Phillip out with you because even if she tries to get you ready for school in the morning she was too weak and tired, he would just send her back to bed.

Late morning when finally woke up she would be energized she usually pick you from school she still didn't understand why she has suddenly develop a sleeping disorder following that we start to notice she would sometimes went on the road without combing her hair she even exclude having a bath daily, she would simple denied it or an excuse how she had forgotten to take a shower.

She continues to sleep in late so one morning when someone from the studio rung the house phone Carter answer I see that he had a perplexed look on his face then he told the person on the other end that he'll be there shortly when he gets off the call he said to me Terry, Celia wasn't in the house she is at the studio they don't have an appointment with her that morning and she told them she was too tired to drive back home they allow her to stay and she had fallen asleep there on a coach, they notice to the changes in her behavior.

They were also aware of her condition because we had informed them and also the places she frequently goes for instance her nail tech, hairdresser, gym and your school we leave number for them to contact us if she turns up and they see where she acting differently.

Phillip was at work so Carter and I went and bring her back home she continues to show up at these places and we continued to go for her.

She was hardly socializing and when she do it was completely off topic so most of the call we received that was the que they would clearly notice to call us.

One morning after she brings you to school she told the teacher that she will wait for school to dismiss the teacher tried to convince her to return home and come back to collect you in a couple hours but she wasn't leaving the teacher call the house, She hadn't ate breakfast so I fix her some and have your grandpa drop me there and we ate the food in her car I asked her why she didn't come back home and her response was the person wanted her to stay, I told her I didn't see anyone else in the parking lot, she told me that's add because he was there with her when I arrived, I talked her into letting me drive her home.

She was still sleeping in the afternoon, I to collect you from school she couldn't do much on her bad days she keep talking to people we couldn't see, but the good ones were a blessing she would cook do laundry takes a bath bring you to school she would do all her regular duties, she would bring you to the park she loves to play dress up with you because it was one of your favorite things to do those days was treasured there was laughter, she even does her rehearsal at the studio and at church when needed, those were memorable times for all of us.

Then there were other times when her illness was acting up it was sad and painful, another hurtful thing we had to do was to take away the key to her car so she could have limited access to the road.

She would carry you to the places that she usually goes to randomly, one day she pick you up from school when hours have passed and she didn't return home, we call her she did answer and let us know that everything was fine, she just wants to spend time with you and visit some new places, she gives us her location she was hours away. When she brought you home that night she was exhausted and you were sleeping and look like a mess all dirty we hid the keys she thought she didn't remember where she had left them and we pretend to not knowing where she put them, we told her we would carry her to wherever she needs to go she was taking some medication that her doctor had prescribed for her but these only makes her weak and wants to sleep all the time, so we prefer to monitor her instead and only when it's really necessary we would give her those meds.

Chapter Eight

A worsening

One morning I went to check on her as that had become a regular thing for me so I can see what condition she was in always hoping it was one of her good days Phillip had left you off at school on his way to work, was I in for a surprise that morning, she had curled up on the sofa talking loudly to herself and both TVs were smashed on the floor. When I got her attention, she told me that people were watching her and giving her instructions and that even when she turned off the television, they were still messing with her head. She said there was too much noise going on inside and that they even told her that they were coming for her. When I get through to her I convince her to come and have some of the breakfast that Carter had prepared and she can tell me more after we have eaten.

Most times give her the calm meds with food and we keep it away from her in the event of an overdose she went back to bed after we ate because she was becoming real drowsy we call your father, he purchased two TV set online to replace those and have the delivery guys install them, but they weren't finish when I pick you up from school so we stop by Kerry's house because you were always excited to play with her kids we stayed for a few hours before your grandpa call to let me know that it's ok to carry you home.

You still stay with your grandpa and me until Phillip return from work because your mommy were sleeping highly sedated those meds causes her to sleep for hours

Many of her songs got airplay regularly she was becoming famous and still most of her fans doesn't even know her silent life. She still did minor interview and a couple of concerts within proximity she was making good money Michael and Karen see to it that her workload was on a minimum and her family see to it that she stay on her medication and doctor visits.

She continues to have flare up days, violently smashing things, talking out loud to herself or the invisible persons, she also takes on a new habit of collecting stuff as a hoarder.

When it had become so frequent we had asked Michael to cancel her studio times for and told Karen don't book her for anything so we put on haul and her public appearances.

It got worse she was causing a fight with Phillip every chance she got without any particular reason.

Then one morning I had just returned from the market when Celia came storming into the kitchen really angry as she approached me I could see that she has blood on her hands and the top she was wearing, frightening I asked her what was going on she wasn't making much sense but from what I gathered it was clear she and Phillip was in a fight again physical this time.

She wasn't the one bleeding when I check on her so I rushed over to their apartment to see Phillip mopping the floor to clean up the blood his hand was in bandage breathing a sigh of relief I took the mop from him, I'll do it better with two hands I had told him, he couldn't use the one that has the bandage so I asked him how bad was it he told me he might need stitches or two. He then brief me on what had happen, Celia was acting up so he was just about to put one of her pills in her juice she come into the kitchen and saw what he was doing she got so upset she start shouting and accuse him of making her sick by giving her poison.

She rush for the knife in the kitchen he tried to take it away from her, and that's how he got cut, she sees the blood got frightened and left

I hastened him to go see the doctor and after I finish cleanup I woke you bring you over to get breakfast too, Celia was still eating your grandpa wink at me I know that he had managed to slip her pill in her food.

After your dad return he comes over to talk to your grandpa and I we were all concerned about Celia conditions she was having relapse more often it was getting scarier because your safety was of uttermost concern, and that was the reason for Phillip coming to us but we weren't ready for his suggestions.

He wants to have her stay in one of those facilities for a few weeks or a few months to see what the outcome would be.

I was totally against it there was no cure for schizophrenia all they would do to her is load her body with drug making her weak and helpless no energy to move around so she will not give problems I told him I'll monitor her more she hasn't reach that far to be lock away we will just have to figure out how to deal with her condition in the meantime.

She still didn't have access to drive she would walk to the nearest store about two blocks away any one of us can drive her to the store, but whenever she is not well she would just walk the community, the park is in walking distance too but the good news is that your school wasn't, it was a ten minutes' drive. Every day was a challenge for all of us but mostly your mother her days was unpredictable days when she was sad and weak, and some days violent and raging, but on her good days she was a loving mother, a kind wife and she wasn't going to give up, she was determined, resilient she kept fighting. There wasn't much for her to do so she start putting stuff on each other she would empty a section of the cupboard and pile it into another section she does the same thing with the clothes your father start to have a difficult time in finding things when he needed it. The things started to pile up in one place and days later she would make a mess having them all over the house and finally putting them away neatly to where they should, it was getting very annoying for Phillip. I try to get her to stay over by me in one of the spare room but she wouldn't and I still held my grounds not to have her institutionalized. It was expected when your dad decided he was going to take you and move in with his mom for some time, he still had the mindset that your mother should be hospitalized but my heart could not allow it the day he was moving he bring Patrick with him and moved all his belongings and most of yours Celia was asleep over by me so she wasn't aware of what was going on. Phillip thought it was better to move and let her know afterwards and I agree he would return when she was awake I decided to have a few close people who support Celia over for a get together because that's the best way we could think of to let them know what's happening Claudette and her husband, were there and also Patrick, Kerry and her kids, Jean, Reverend and his wife had come too. There was food and drinks when she awoke and freshen up your dad take her and have a private conversation with her and after Reverent and his wife had a talk with them also when they return you could see that she was crying, but throughout the course of the evening she kept it together for your sake although I don't think you would notice because you were having a blast with Kerry kids. When it was time to eat the Reverend had bless the table, we all ate and have a somewhat good time, later when everything was over and they all left, Jean told us that she would have stayed the night with your mother to keep her company. Before Carter and I retired to bed they both were still up curling up on the couch watching horror movies I smiled to myself and said it was not all lost she will have the support of her close family and friends that morning the four of us had breakfast before Jean left for work. It was the weekend and she wanted to get her hair done so I bring her to the hairdresser afterwards we went to the mall, because she needs to do some shopping she was always buying things for you and that day was no exception. She had purchased a lot of clothes for you, I think she was replacing those your father had taken, she included a lot of church dresses, one of the agreements that she and your dad has, is for you to attend church each Sunday. If Phillip won't be at church that day he would drop you off at the house or his mother would do it. Carter was asleep when we reaches the house, he wasn't feeling well himself lately, age was a factor for that sooner or later it catches up on us, so I told Celia that I will take a nap myself and she told me that she feels the need to do some writing for a few hours. I urge her to move over again but she said she will think about it but for now she need the alone time to focus she left and promise to be back later that evening for dinner. I text her when dinner was almost ready, when she walk into the kitchen she was carrying a sheet of paper I ask her how the words was coming on she told me that the song was finish, I was impress she had just take a few hours to complete her song she wanted me to hear it I stop what I was doing to give her my full attention while she was about half way through it your grandpa walk in while listening to the words I couldn't help water fill my eyes it was a happy and a tearful song but in the end the words were. The joy in my sadness is to know that you're happy and you could feel it, she had to accept the present she had given up control of the outcome and she was at peace with it. Tears were now running down her face both Carter and I went over and hugged her and we cry it was tears of bonding, of love, of peace, of acceptance, of strength, of uncertainty, it was tears of complete release. After dinner we video chat with you and Claudette we didn't see Phillip and his name wasn't mentioned later when we were retiring for bed she was still watching television but promise that she will just sleep over for the night with us. On Sunday a few minutes before we leave out for church your dad bring you by he wasn't attending church that day but told us he will be back later to pick you up he kisses you then hug Celia before he left, you then look up at both of them with a bright smile on your face. The service was lovely as the day was, it was late spring, summer was just around the corner, the sun was out, light breeze a cool day, but it was a different atmosphere in church after your mother had finished singing the song that she had just wrote no one could sit down the Holy Spirit was in control members were in a praise and worship energy inside the church was hot it was amazing. Later that evening Celia and you meet up with Kerry and her kids at the park you were excited when you reach home because Kerry had taken you all to have ice cream. when your father come by for you he stayed for a while to talk with your mother about what sort of plan she has if any because your birthday was in a few weeks the year before there wasn't a big plan because Celia was busy with her music tour so she had it catered in your class at school which was very special and you didn't mind where it kept as long as there was cake, presents and kids to play with. They had both agree on keeping it at church they were going to keep it a surprise, there was a lot of children attending church and they have the available space in the Sunday school area and quite a number of parents kept their child party there also. After you and your dad left she told me she was going to talk to Michael and have him listen to the song and see if he would have allowed her to come into the studio, I know that wouldn't be a problem because the song was amazing four days later I was with her for most of the morning my intentions was to bring her there and go back for her she asked if I want to stay and watch her I was happy to stay with her I've never being there with her before Phillip had gone a few times but she would mostly went by herself, later when she was finished it was time to pick you up from school, Claudette and your dad wasn't available so days like this I was responsible in picking you up. On our way there she talk more about what they will be doing to get her song release most of what she said I didn't even understand but I listen she know I was supporting her, we pick you up afterwards we stop by the pharmacy for her to collect her refills. I stay in the car with you while she rushes in, you want to know why she went inside, about to celebrate your seventh birthday, you started to take notice, you were curious, you have an unanswered question and you want to understand what was happening. I briefly explained to you that she was very ill and she had to take medication constant for now, you then wanted to know when will she be better because you want to come back home, the best I could think of was the doctor didn't know as yet, but Celia comes into the car at the same time and nothing more was said.

When we arrived at the house she suggest that the two of you watch one of your favorite movies, she was feeling tired and she had taken some pain pills after leaving the studio, I was thinking that help causes her to feel drowsy, she know she would fall asleep shortly but she would be there with you. You both talk for a little, while curl up on the couch not long after she fall asleep beside you.

I was outside sitting on the patio watching Carter and the gardener out when you come and sit beside me, you then call my name when I turned on look at you there was concern in your eyes as was earlier when we were in the car i could see that you need more answers so I told you to go ahead and talk I'm listening, you told me your father talk about your mommy and said that she was really sick, because it was unsafe for them to live with her that is the reason they have to moved and lived with grandma Claudette, but why she still live with me and grandpa why did we stay.

\At that moment I realized that your mother legacy needs to be preserved not only the pictures or videos but momentum is for you to learn of later when you are older to understand. I went inside for some ice cream for you and talk some more of what was going on leaving out the name schizophrenia and it is meaning.

We went inside to finish watching the movie together while your mother slept.

The rest of the week went by with no major hiccups Celia and I accompanied her to the studio to finish her recording so she could have it release, I didn't have any more days to pick you up. One afternoon after school he brought you by the house so you could spend a few hours with your mom, but when it was time to leave you become rebellious and start to cry reality start to sink in, you started missing your mom and your home.

You were shouting at your dad that you want to come back home this was expected they just have to be patient Celia had to try and convince you that it was ok she going to get well soon, she got you to calm down trying to reassure you that you will be coming back home, she also got you distracted by reminding you that your birthday was coming up and she was planning on something special which is a surprise, this shift your focus she become loving and caring and you become quiet and listen to her she hugs and kisses you and eventually you leave with your dad.

We see you a few days later when your father bring you to church he then come by the house and we have dinner together after he had left with you.

Jean come by she and Celia went to the movies, the morning I awoke just in time to see them heading out to go to the gym it was really nice to see that she allowed Celia to drive.

Phillip, Carter and I allowed her to drive sometimes but we don't let her get on the road by herself that week was busy she was helping the young people prepared for youth Sunday so for that weekend your grandfather and I or Jean has to transport her around.

The following weekend would be your birthday so she basically was getting as much things in place as possible while she was spending the time at Church organizing the concert it went well, because that Sunday the young people were responsible for conducting the service, the adult prepared food so it was a full day of activities and food When it had finished and we left the church it was too late to come by the house so your father take you home.

It was an enjoyable day Celia had you most of the time she didn't have much preparation to do in the upcoming week for your birthday party just to confirm the orders for the cake, decorate the Sunday school area and put the ice cream in the refrigerator.

I had also pick you up that Friday after school so you could stay with us until the Sunday after church your birthday was actually the Saturday and Celia, you, Jean, Kerry and her kids went to the movies after you return you got open some presents.

I guess you believe that was it you were totally blown away when you go to church and Sunday school kids surprise you when you see all the decorations and the cakes and lots of presents. It was service as usual for the adult but you got to spend a couple of hours to enjoy yourself with the kids your dad and mommy and also grandma Claudette, later Carter and I look at the pictures and watch the videos of your party.

Weeks went by and the only sign with your mom was a few blank out, irregular headaches and hoarding in her apartment then one evening Kerry call to ask her if she was interested in hanging out at the park for a little while, she had agreed and left the house to meet her there when she was there waiting Kerry call her back to let her know that something has come up so she is canceling, she now as to walk back she was near to the corner store so she went there to get something to drink, we don't know what really transpired but from what I heard she was leaving the store without paying for the drink, we see to it that she had always have a small amount of cash her phone and an identification someone tries to stop her when she was walking out without paying she pushed him away and he landed onto the selves damage some goods nothing major, the person received some minor bruises and decided not to press charges.

The store owner had called the cops by then Celia was inpatient so when they arrived she didn't want to go with them they saw the situation in the store thought she was on hard drugs and they use force to restrain her.

I received a call from the police I was utterly frightened and confused when I heard who was on the other end and was asking me if I had known her, he told me to come by the station.

I didn't understand what was going on because she was supposed to be with Kerry and her kids Carter were driving I was too nervous to go behind the wheel, I called Kerry then, that's when I find out she didn't meet with her, she explained when she called to cancel she thought Celia was still at the house.

I didn't call Phillip I had to call him after I get more information when we arrived they refer me to the arresting cop he outline the incident and I explained that she had been diagnosed with schizophrenia, he said he could see that there was something going on with her, he also explained that the store owner will not press charges either as long as we pay for the damaged goods we were fine with that.

The police statements still stand and she will have to go to a court hearing and the need of an evaluation from a therapist for court hearing, if the state should be able to have her charges drop so they are keeping her locked up overnight and prepare paperwork to have her hospitalized for an evaluation report.

They informed us that she was physically ok and we could see her briefly, I had a breakdown when I see her she was so gone, in her eyes she looks so wild, so weak I don't even know if she recognizes us, Carter and I was talking to her but not once did she respond.

The cop told us he will inform us where they would take her in the morning so we could go see her we call Phillip after leaving the police station and walk him through what had happen but decided not to tell anyone else until the following day when we know which facilitates they have sent her.

After Phillip had brought you to school that day he stops at the house, by then we know which hospital they had taken your mother to when we arrived they had admit her on the psyche ward we had to wait awhile for them to finish their evaluation of her when we finally get the chance to see her she was in a tiny room dress in white and lying in bed, she seems drain weak and disoriented the entire time we were there she didn't say anything and we try to get her to talk but the only response she would nod her head she was trying not to fall asleep by forcing her eyes to stay open, it was impossible being that heavily sedated I told her to close her eyes and get some rest, we will take the best care of her princess until she gets better and come home her eyes blinked in return and in no time she was sound asleep all four of us left it was Claudette Phillip Carter and I.

Your dad didn't go to work that day so he collect you when school was dismissed and come by the house so he could explain to you that your mother was in the hospital it was a challenging day for him, and one of my worst day I have to make a couple of uncomfortable calls, the worst yet is calling her mother she breaks down over the phone I told her most of what was going on with Celia at that time and she will be making arrangements to visit her if needed.

We visited her the following day she was in the same room she didn't seem that drugged but she was talking about the events of the past, she was as if on happy pills a euphoria she was just skipping from one story to another we go along with it and when we were leaving she was so calm kissing and hugging and so excited like a child she was waving goodbye and smiling, we then meet with the doctor for her evaluation report he wasn't going to discharge her as yet because he needed to monitor her illnesses with her medication and at that point he cannot give us a specific day for her release a feeling of hopelessness, we couldn't ignore the fact knowing that you could be without your mother for days or even weeks.

Because Of your age couldn't visit her, it wasn't allowed they also have limited visitors rules but everyone would send their hello, most times she wouldn't even recall who was who on the matter she was mostly sedated and so it happens days become weeks and before we knew it she was there over a month Phillip visiting becomes less and his excuses become more but our main focus and hope was for your mother to get better and come home to be with you, her family and friends.

Her mother was making arrangements to come stay for a few months when she was released for her help and support it was two months and she was still in the facilities when Phillip come by the house one morning after leaving you at school he wants to talk to Carter and I there was no doubt this was a different kind of conversation because from the moment he showed up I notice he wasn't wearing his wedding band neither was Celia but she wasn't allowed to wear any form of jewelry as a patient where she is at.

We decided to have a sit and listen to what he have to say it was a lot most of what we understand and some of what we were expecting and then some of it surprising he had drawn up divorce paper a month before, expecting her to have been home by then to sign them but now he is considering to bring them to her there to get her signatures, he had make arrangements to move to Canada to live with his son mother and they are planning on getting married as soon as the divorce is finalized, so he need to get it started when I asked him about you he told me that he had spoken with his lawyer and there shouldn't be any problem due to the fact that Celia wasn't capable of taking care of you and she isn't in any condition to contest him getting full custody and he had also get you in school there already.

He continued to talk about having me sign over your legacy as part beneficiary and co-sign for Celia trust fund so he could save it for you because he won't be carrying you back or sending you to visit as long as Celia is in that condition and how recovery seems hopeless, he needs to take you from an environment that might have a mental and emotional effect on you.

We know that certainly things were out of our hands where you were concerned he was your parent and Celia was in fact out of the picture, whereas making decisions of your wellbeing but the way he was going about everything as if Celia was dead.

I guess to him she already was, I wasn't pleased with his attitude and I wasn't going to fight with him, but I know for certain that he will not bring a divorce paper to have her sign in that place, with whatever progress she was making to be reversed.

I let him know whatever signing I'm going to do will be done when your mother is released, he then may have her sign the papers.

He agreed to my terms he told me that you will be out of school for the upcoming week until your flight on Thursday, but he is ok in having you spend from Sunday when he brings you by for church, until Wednesday to stay with us I accept it with enthusiasm.

I don't know when again I'll see you if ever after Wednesday I try to reason with him to have you stay throughout the rest of the school term at least but his mind as being made up I thought that his plan was in the making for some time because he had it all planned out so then it would be the opportunity to have my sister change her flight arrangements so I make the call and talk to her for some time to give her a heads up on what is son in law is about to do it was a few days before Sunday so I told her I get her on a flight to be here by the end of the week so she can also get to spend time with you before your dad take you away you were her only grandchild presently and like her we were going to miss you with our whole heart she took the news really hard but she decided she wouldn't miss the time to spend with you for nothing else in the world so we book her to arrives Saturday afternoon.

Chapter Nine

A forever goodbye

arter and I went for her at the airport and from there we went straight to the hospital to see Celia your grandma couldn't help it she broke down right in front of her she sat on the bed with your mother crying Celia was comforting her by hugging her and telling her it's going to be alright.

I left the room so they could spend some time with each other and went with Carter to see her doctor, we talk with him about what was happening with her family and to our surprise he also have some startling news that was completely nerve wracking he had a plan to tell us the following Monday because they are waiting on some more result but since we were already with him he might as well let us know that your mother has stage four cancer of the brain, which was the cause of some of her actions and pains she was having with her been schizophrenic and the medication it was a distraction for the cancer getting worse, if he had picked up on it in its early stage they might have the advantage to operate and cure her, but it's too late now he also mention that on Monday when we visit he will be discharging her so we will be able to spend some time with her because time for her is counting down rapidly.

We went back to her room with her doctor and he repeat what he had just told us in front of her and her mother more crying, it was going to be a long weekend, as from then on out things will never be the same.

We left the hospital a few hours later we were all drain exhausted we had a light dinner and turn in for bed early your grandma has to take some meds to relieve her headache and put her to sleep.

On Sunday when your dad bring you by he sees that Celia's mother was there I didn't tell him she was coming he was frightened in giving a hasty retreat she didn't pay much attention to him she was just happy to see you and grateful that she will have a few days before you left she was awfully sad about everything that was going on, especially with everything that her daughter has to endure the pain of losing her family and dealing with the fact that the doctor said she has limited time, because there is nothing they can do with or about her cancer.

We didn't even worry to say anything to Phillip it doesn't even matter now that he is leaving in a few days it was up to your mother to tell him if she wanted to we went to church as plan Reverend and the congregation pray for her and on Monday her friend Jean and I went to the hospital for her she was released with a lot of medications and little and no hope.

A few family friends was there to welcome her home with gifts and a cheerful atmosphere we had told Claudette and your dad that Celia was coming home when we were on the way to pick her up and they both stop by the house everyone was friendly in conversation and laughter right until they all left she and Phillip didn't talk much he didn't come by Tuesday until Wednesday when he showed up with the divorce papers for her to sign they were over by her apartment and you were with us after a few hours they both joined us and it was clear that they both were crying She told us later that she let him know about the cancer and he had left the papers and told her she should feel free to sign it whenever she wants to he won't rush anything, he also told her that he had to leave because his new job begins the upcoming week but she should keep you for the rest of the term which is less than two months, and he will make the necessary arrangements about school and come back and get you when school is on break, she was delighted and so was the rest of us.

She had lost a lot of weight and she continues to lose more some days were long and some nights too because she was in so much pain and she tries to cope without meds, especially when you're home because it only left her sleepy and weak over the next couple weeks she would muster all the energy and strength to be with you and to have fun so you can make more happy memories and be able to remember your last days together.

There were only two mishaps in between one she had gotten angry at you when you went into bedroom one morning to tell her you need breakfast she shouted at you to get out of her room and get your dad to fix it for you when you told her that your dad wasn't there she shouted at you again to get out, your grandma heard you crying because she was still sleeping and didn't know you were up so she tries to get you to calm and fix your favorite breakfast which was egg sandwich and hot chocolate we give her the meds with her breakfast and have her sleep it off and when she was awake we told her what had happened, she was sad she apologized to you, telling you how much she loves you, you meant the world to her, you will forever be the best thing that had happened in her life, how special you were and you must always remember that, she got her friend bring you all to the movies later, her treat.

The other incident happens somewhat more tragic you both had just finished playing dress up and was about to watch a movie in her room, she pick you up to put you on the bed and she just fell with you in her arms, both of you were still on the floor when your grandmother rush into the room she pick you up and check if you were alright there was nothing seems wrong with you, but your mother wasn't moving and it can't be from the fall only, because she did fell on the carpet and although your grandma was doing everything to get her respond, she wasn't she then rush over by my apartment when I get to Celia's room she was still unresponsive but she was breathing when I check her pulse so I call emergency number and a few minutes later they have her in the ambulance and on their way to the hospital, she was rush to the emergency but there wasn't anything they could do but to stabilized her heartbeat she was in a semi coma for the next two days and family friends visited her and the second day early in the morning we received a call from the hospital that we should come in and so we got the news that she sleep away her cancer had finally won.

A few days later we keep a service at our church your dad had attended but her final resting place is to have her buried in the family plot beside her father back home in two weeks.

Phillip gave us the ok to bring you but when we return to the state he will come for you it was mourning for the days and weeks following up to our final goodbyes, with a lot of condolences from her former co-workers in the health industry, the music industry and the church family some even take a trip to pay their final respect to her by attending the service we kept in Jamaica among them were Reverent and his wife and Claudette and her husband and Jean and Celia's manager.

After returning, I get the chance to really look through the shoe box your mother had left we found it when we were going through her stuff we decided to pack up her things and donate them and the rest sent to Jamaica since your grandma was there to help sort them out that box was a memoir present from her to you and four envelopes one letter to each one of us, your father, you, her mother, one for me and carter she also left a note to have me keep your letter and the stuff in the box until you are old enough to understand.

My Phillip dearest,

I will always love you. We had gotten married young and for both of us it was a test and trial period. Sometimes we didn't see eye to eye, issues happen, we get upset at each other, and there were days when we felt disappointed, burdensome, confused bumping heads we even felt like failures.

We did ride the waves the good times precede, the memories had relieved, I had hoped things would have been better, but we didn't do all badly.

But through it all we have always one thing right and that's our daughter, she was the glue in our relationship, when everything else seems gloomy, she was definitely the love of both of our lives.

We both can agree that our Ashia was one of the most meaningful reasons of our union, my love we created life.

They were the days when emotionally, mentally and physically I felt numb, but the will to be present for her was the only energy that keeps me going. I know without a doubt you will do your best to raise our baby girl you're the best dad she could ever asked for. I hope you keep her in my family lives that she know and connect with them and keep that relationship also. We have form a support team with the church too and one day I hope she revisit.

I just want to say I'm sorry for not being a different kind of woman, the kind that was healthy mentally and physically. I am sorry I had to leave our daughter for you to raise by yourself and I also apologize for any resentment that you might have against me

Love Always,
Celia

Dear Ashia,

My beautiful Angel, how I wish that I could stay around to watch you grow and blossom into this wonderful woman I know you have become.

I had dreams of you every day some are simple while others are important, others sad and some happy times when I either scold are encourages you

I had dreams of you attending school from kindergarten, high school and college, selecting friends and participating in groups. I had dreams of being at all of your events.

I had dreams of you having crush on guys and dating, I have dreams of taking pictures and recordings at your graduation.

I had dreams of you chosen the career that you want, that fills your soul.

I even have dreams of my grandkids, yes you creating a loving family of your own with a husband who loves you unconditionally.

My baby you are special you are wonderfully and beautifully design, created with that purpose in life. My days were bearable because you were my reason for breathing, you were my kryptonite, I looked forward to my days just to be with you

Ashia I will always be with you, If at any time you feel lonely or sad, put your arm on your heart beat you feel it's real that's how real and alive my love is for you my baby.

Love Always,
Mommy

Dear mother,

I know how you must be feeling, I have seen how losing our dad has taken a toll on you. It was months before I see your smile again and beneath it anyone could see your loneliness.

I know how it feels to know that that person is leaving will be gone forever.

When I had migrated although we were apart we look forward to the day when we will see each other, me leaving you all behind had torn my heart into pieces and it ache more each and every day. But I want you to promise me you will take care of yourself, cry when you feel to but learn to make peace and be present in the lives of your other children, gain strength from them allowed them to be your rock they are young and strong and capable to help carry you through this time.

Mommy you have done your best, you have raised good kids, they will take care of you, you will live to see and be happy with your grandchildren. Ashia one day will find you and her aunts, uncles and cousin again.

I asked you not to have any regrets of losing me, I was always in so much pain, death was the only relieved I see at times, wherever I am going I am sure I will be relieved of this pain in my body. I love you with all my heart, I will always be watching over you.

Love Always,
Celia

Dear Aunt Terri and Uncle Carter,

I were lucky, how many people get the opportunity to get two set of wonderful parents in their lifetime.

I remember the day when you pick me up at the airport, to tell you the truth I was telling myself that I was dreaming from I board the plane back home, I was asking myself is it real am I going to be living with you be able to get the opportunity to accomplish more than what my life at that moment was giving me.

I wasn't going to believe until I see you, that the time I allowed it reality to sink in. You were amazing in how you support me in every way possible. You had entered my life right in a moment when I was transforming into adulthood and it was a time that I was grateful to have the experience with you.

I was a strain sometimes but never once have I seen or felt that you see me as a burden. Days when I know that I was out of control, I felt awful because you have lost your son and his family suddenly tragically and somehow I felt I was causing the same stress but this time you felt you were losing me slowly tragically, and it pains my heart, but I find comfort in the fact that if time should repeat you and Uncle Carter would do it all again.

I love you and I hope you find comfort in knowing I am going to a better place, until we meet again.

Love Always,
Celia

Epilogue

Mrs Daniels your visitor is here. Ok I'm all set nurse Wright, where is he?

Patrick, I'm right here Mrs Daniels I have to carry the bag for you Therrisa, Patrick three days clothes is not a lot that an old lady can't manage, I don't even need a wheelchair to take me to the car in the parking lot but nurse Wright here said its procedure, she would hear me out although I kept telling her that you might think that me being in a chair is too old for you and would be a bother at your house this holiday.

Mrs Daniels you're joking right, because for the past three years you have been spending Thanks Giving with us and you haven't aged a bit and if you can't make it to my house, well then me, my wife and the three boys will be coming here, lol so are you ready to rock and roll

Theresa ...Please give me a second I have to wait on Nurse Wright to push me to the car (finger expression)...So call procedure right...both laughing. Patrick can I say something to you

Knock on the door...Therrisa speaking come in no one enter but there was a knock again, Theresa who was closest to the door turn the door knob and open it. Shock she steer, she blinks a couple of times to see if her eyes were fooling her, it wasn't standing there was the same eyes from over a decade ago the and without a words tears started to run down her face

Ashia...walk over with eyes clouded with tears ... yes it is me, grandma, Its Ashia, I'm here she hugged her and Theresa wrap her arms around her as tightly as she could whispering in her ears she said i know without a doubt that I would live to see you again, because I have asked God and I know he was going to deliver on his promise

Theresa turn to Patrick who by now was sitting on the only chair that was in the room, do you know about this she said ...but instantly she catch upon herself, of course you do you both come here together in your in on this surprise how long now? She asked

Patrick gave a slight chuckle since her birthday two months ago, Theresa look from him to Ashia she also gave her a shy grin and a nod Patrick continued to speak and yes she is going to keep you for a few days or so but what stays the same is you guys gonna have Thanksgiving with my family . But there is a lot more to discuss a lot of catching up and a few more surprises so let's go

Most of the residents there know she was leaving for a few days some already left with family members with another brief goodbye, see you in three are four days left. She knows where Patrick lived before she left to live in the assisted living home she went there a couple of times for special occasion baby christening, birthday party, special holidays etc. After a few minutes he told her that they were going to Ashia's place, and he will come to get them tomorrow for Thanksgiving

For the forty mins drive to the house Ashia was question her and how she was doing if the staff treated her well if they make her felt comfortable if she enjoyed living there she basically wants to get hands on of her well-being and Theresa was happy in all areas, because no one basically put her there it was something she had done her research on with carter before he died they have consciously started putting things in place after their son died and readjust and make some changes to it over the years. After he passes she had went there herself after shopping around she had decided on that one

Theresa …. I know this area she was saying looking out the window as they drive, turning her head to look back at Asia don't tell me we are going to our old house.

Ashia … no, she lol if it was available but would you want that grandma, I meant to say there again.

Theresa… no; too much memories that would bring up emotions that my old age just can't manage

Shortly after Patrick pull into a nice driveway a newly two story house, all the houses were new about a dozen a recently developed housing settlement. Home he said and instantly she have that flashback with Celia hopping out of the car and running towards the front door. Ashia open the driver's door holding her hand she help her out while Patrick takes out a wheelchair and her suitcase

Ashia … will you be needed the wheelchair grandma there is a ramp or you rather walk. She told her she could walk, occasionally she uses the wheelchair

When the get inside they got her settled in a suite on the ground floor, Patrick then left, promise to call later to check on them and Ashia slowly show around the house which is a three bedroom condo upstairs houses her lovely studio with a lookout view which they went to last.

Theresa was in awe her she was impress her work was lovely as she walked around she showed her newest project she will be working on months down the line she had blowed up some of the memoirs in the box from photos, scenery, trinkets and promise to create a whole collection

Theresa was overwhelmed they look beautiful she was delighted that she finally figure it out, from Celia sickness she had created some of the loveliest music and now her daughter is creating and bringing to life the loveliest art.

The cycle of life shines beauty on every street, in ever rivers, in every valley, it never stops but we don't always see it because we are limited or blinded by our physical vision but putting the spiritual lens on and be amazed, it is a whole new world

When the day was over they went shopping at whole food store that is Theresa friendly. They had cooked a lovely dinner and was relaxing comfortable in the living area having a light conversation with each other trying to take it slow in learning as much as possible of the missing years in so doing releasing and absorbing energy of different emotions that was in the room

Ashia .... Grandmother I would love if you lived with me, I moved back here to live one like the weather better here. Also I am in the middle I can visit my mom relatives in Jamaica and my dad relatives in Canada but my main reason for being here is to take care of you

Theresa .... Are you sure I can still do a lot for myself but time will come when it is going to be all on you, you know that right could you manage I wouldn't want to cause such stress on you and remember you're pretty young, you shouldn't have to be worrying about me right now is the time to be making friends male and female going on dates enjoying your youth ...But i would wish for nothing more than to spend my last days with you. Thanks Ashia

Ashia .... Grandma Ther all that you just said won't stop me from doing what you mention from me having you with me here, there is a lot more years for me to start babysit you and as for help when that time comes I will get the help to continue to take care of you, you are the mother I have never have and my mom would have wanted me to do this. But most importantly I am doing this because of me you have giving me a part of my life I would have missed out on, the part I would never get an answer I would have that gap that would never be filled it is the least I could for the most amazing gift I ever received. I am the one should be thanking you

Then her phone ring it was Patrick, what is the verdict, he said yes Ashia answer, she had answer it on speaker Patrick and her wife was laughing and clapping. I am happy that she decided to stay Hopeful was saying I needed her help in discipline these two that Patick is spoiling

Theresa …. Give a day or two with them and they will be calling me mean grandma

Hopepal … Hi Theresa didn't know you were hearing, that's right, I will be taking you up on the offer which I doubt will happen because Ashia will be against I don't think she will letting you out of her site ever again, I can't wait to see you tomorrow. Have a good night's sleep. Bye

Theresa and Ashia…… Good Night Patrick, Good night Hopepal

Later that night, she had just finished praying and was ready for bed Ashia tap on the door and pushed it open Grandma I am happy you decided to stay we will go by the residence and collect your things the day after tomorrow, I promise I will make you being here with me as comfortable as possible you won't be disappointed

Theresa … I believe you I have heard it before for once I had never been disappointed and I will play might part in making this our home happy . I love you Ashia

Ashia …walking over to her hug her I love you too, sleep well your home Grandma. Tomorrow is a new day, I have so much to tell you, but first on my list is to give you all the details about my trip to Jamaica and Sunday coming we will be attending church, I had added all my mommy wishes to my bucket list…Goodnight

She reaches the door and stop turn around and whispered thanks for the gift

Printed in the United States
By Bookmasters